The longest eclipse of the Sun ever recorded is 7 minutes and 8 seconds. It was seen from the Philippines, in 1955.

The highest wind speed ever recorded in a tornado measured 278 miles per hour.

Greenland is the world's biggest island. It has an area of 840,000 square miles.

The oldest rock which has been dated scientifically is 3,800 million years old.

The world's deepest lake is Lake Baykal in central Siberia, Russia. Its deepest part is 6,364 feet below the surface.

The world's strongest currents are the Nakwakto Rapids, Slingsby Channel, in Canada. Their flow speed is sometimes as high as 18 miles per hour.

The longest glacier is the Lambert Glacier in Australian Antarctic Territory. It measures at least 248 miles in length, and is 40 miles across at its widest point.

The world's highest waterfalls are the Angel Falls, Venezuela. From top to bottom they measure 3,212 feet.

The widest waterfalls are the Khône Falls in Laos. They are about 65 feet high, but nearly 7 miles wide.

The world's shortest river is the D River in Oregon, USA. It connects Devil's Lake to the Pacific Ocean, and is 439 feet long at low tide.

The largest underground cavern is the Sarawak Chamber in Gunung Mulu National Park, in Sarawak. It is 2,300 feet long, has an average width of 980 feet, and its height is never less than 230 feet.

The deepest mine is the Western Deep Gold Mine in South Africa. It is 12,467 feet deep.

The biggest diamond ever found is the Cullinan Diamond. It was discovered in South Africa in 1905, and weighed more than 1 pound.

How many more world records can you find in this book?

**LAKESIDE JOINT SCHOOL
DISTRICT**

19621 BLACK ROAD

LOS GATOS, CALIFORNIA 95030

TELEPHONE (408) 354-2372

THE PHYSICAL WORLD

THE PHYSICAL WORLD

By Tony Seddon and Jill Bailey

Doubleday & Company, Inc., Garden City, New York

This book was designed and produced by
BLA Publishing Limited,
East Grinstead, Sussex, England.
A member of the Ling Kee Group
LONDON · HONG KONG · TAIPEI · SINGAPORE · NEW YORK

ISBN: 0-385-24179-8

Contents

Acknowledgements/Picture Credits

The publishers wish to thank the following people and organizations for their invaluable assistance in the preparation of this book:

British Petroleum
Shell
Solid Fuel Advisory Service

ARTISTS:

David Anstey; Kevin Diaper; Paul Doherty; Keith Duran/Linden Artists; Fiona Fordyce; George Fryer/Linden Artists; Helen Kennett; Alan Male/Linden Artists; Karen Moxon; Sallie Alane Reason; Rosie Vane-Wright; Brian Watson/Linden Artists.

PHOTOGRAPHIC CREDITS
t = top; *b* = bottom; *c* = centre; *l* = left; *r* = right.

COVER: S. Jonasson/Frank Lane Picture Agency.
11/12 ZEFA. 14 Frank Lane Picture Agency. 15*t* G.I. Bernard/OSF. 15*l* Geoscience Features. 15*r* ZEFA. 16 Science Photo Library. 17*l* Frank Lane Picture Agency. 17*r*, 18 ZEFA. 19 Jill Bailey. 20 John Lythgoe/Seaphot. 21 J.G. James/Seaphot. 22*t* Frank Lane Picture Agency. 22*b* Michael Fogden/OSF. 23, 24, 25*b* Geoscience Features. 25*t* Vincent Serventy/Seaphot. 26, 27 ZEFA. 28 Mansell Collection. 29 Frank Lane Picture Agency. 30 Phil Chapman/Seaphot. 31 Chris Howes/Seaphot. 33*t* Science Photo Library. 33*b* Novosti Press Agency. 35 Geoscience Features. 36*l* Science Photo Library. 36*r* Robert Hessler/Seaphot. 37 Roberto Bunge/Seaphot. 38 Frank Lane Picture Agency. 39*t* Ivor Edmunds/ Seaphot. 39*b* Geoscience Features. 41*t* Michael Fogden/OSF. 41*b* David Rootes/ Seaphot. 42 Frank Lane Picture Agency. 43 ZEFA. 45*t* Frank Lane Picture Agency. 45*b* South American Pictures. 46, 47*l* ZEFA. 47*r* Gillian Lythgoe/Seaphot. 49*l* Frank Lane Picture Agency. 49*r* Michael Fogden/OSF. 50 Robin Buxton/OSF. 51 Science Photo Library. 52*t* David Wrigglesworth/OSF. 52*b* ZEFA. 53 Anthony Bannister/OSF. 54*t* Michael Fogden/OSF. 54*b* Anthony Bannister/OSF. 56*t* M. Ogilvie/Seaphot. 56*b* Frank Lane Picture Agency. 57 Geoscience Features. 58 Alastair Shay/OSF. 59 Geoscience Features. 60*l* Antony Joyce/Seaphot. 60*r*, 61*l* ZEFA. 61*r* Geoff Harwood/Seaphot. 62*l* Ivor Edmunds/Seaphot. 62*r* John Lythgoe/Seaphot. 63*t*, 63*b*, 64*l* Geoscience Features. 64*r*, 65 Peter Scoones/Seaphot. 67, 69*t* ZEFA. 69*b* Nancy Sefton/Seaphot. 72*t*, 72*b* Gillian Lythgoe/Seaphot. 73*t* Ed Lawrenson. 73*b* ZEFA. 74*t*, 74*b* Richard Chesher/Seaphot. 75 Leroy F. Grant/Seaphot. 76 Richard Matthews/Seaphot. 77*tl* Tresco Abbey Gardens. 77*tr* Frank Lane Picture Agency. 77*b* Keith Scholey/Seaphot. 78 Science Photo Library. 81 ZEFA. 84 Science Photo Library. 85 Frank Lane Picture Agency. 88, 90 Science Photo Library. 91*l* ZEFA. 91*r* Ivor Edmunds/Seaphot. 93, 95 ZEFA. 96 Frank Lane Picture Agency. 97, 101 ZEFA. 105 NASA. 107 Douglas Dickins. 110 Peter Scoones/Seaphot. 111*l* Solid Fuel Advisory Service. 111*r* ZEFA. 112 British Museum/Natural History. 113 Shell. 114, 115*t*, 115*b* ZEFA. 118 Philippa Scott/NHPA. 119 British Petroleum. 120 Science Photo Library. 121, 123*l* ZEFA. 123*r* South American Pictures. 125 John Lythgoe/ Seaphot. 126 ZEFA. 127 John Lythgoe/Seaphot. 129 Richard Matthews/Seaphot. 130, 131 ZEFA. 133*l* National Coal Board. 133*r* ZEFA. 135 Science Photo Library. 137 NASA. 138 Science Photo Library. 139 NASA/Science Photo Library. 140*l* NASA/ Seaphot. 140*r*, 141*t*, 141*b* NASA. 142*l* John Mason. 142*r*, 143 Science Photo Library. 144 ZEFA. 145 Science Photo Library.

Introduction

The Earth on which we live is a strange and unique planet. It is roughly spherical in shape, but not quite. It weighs about 6000 million million million tons, and its surface occupies more than 193 million square miles, two thirds of which is covered by water. In comparision to some of the other planets in our solar system, the Earth is quite small. But it would still take you more than 250 days to walk around the equator — assuming you walked at normal walking speed and that you walked continually without stopping.

Our planet was formed about 4600 million years ago, and scientists are still arguing about how it first came into existence. As far as we know, it is the only planet in our solar system which is able to support life. Since its formation, the Earth has been changing all the time and it is still changing, even to-day. Humans have existed on its surface for only a short time. But we are curious animals, and our curiousity and sense of adventure have led us to investigate more and more about our planet home. We have managed to travel to most parts of the Earth, from the highest mountain to the deepest part of the sea, from the hottest desert to the coldest pole. More recently we have even traveled beyond our Earth's boundary and ventured into space.

Our knowledge of planet Earth grows every day, and we are finding out new things all the time. Scientists think that the Earth will continue to exist for at least another 5000 million years, so there is plenty of time for you to find out more about the Earth, the way it is made, and how it works. This book has been written to help you achieve this. We hope it will also encourage you to ask more questions about your planet home and to find the answers you want.

Note to the reader
On page 152 of this book you will find the glossary. This gives brief explanations of words which may be new to you.

The Earth

The Earth beneath your feet

Have you ever wondered what the Earth is like beneath your feet. If you could travel right through the center of the Earth to the other side, what would you find on the way?

The Earth is rather like an onion; it is made up of several layers. The outermost layer is the crust, which is made up of solid rock. The crust is very thin, rather like a skin.

Under the crust is the mantle. The mantle is much denser and heavier than the crust. The inner part of the mantle is a strange substance, neither truly solid nor truly liquid. It is often described as "plastic." This is semi liquid rock, the sort that is thrown up as lava by volcanoes. Slow currents move the mantle rocks.

Deeper still, we come to the core. The outer part of the core is made of molten liquid rock containing a lot of iron and nickel, very dense and very heavy. Deeper still, the core becomes solid and even more dense.

▼ Inside the planet Earth.

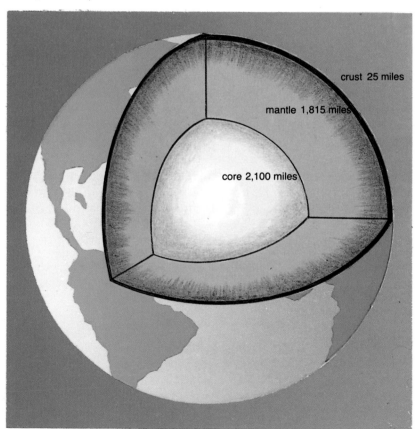

crust 25 miles

mantle 1,815 miles

core 2,100 miles

The living planet

The Earth is the only planet in our solar system which we know can support life. It has an atmosphere for breathing, liquid water, and a temperature which is neither too hot nor too cold for living creatures. Although the Earth produces some heat from chemical reactions in its core, most of its heat comes from the Sun, 93 million miles away.

The spinning Earth

The Earth is not a perfect sphere. It bulges at the equator, and is slightly flattened at the poles.

Imagine a line drawn from the North Pole to the South Pole through the center of the Earth. This is the Earth's axis. The Earth spins around on its axis all the time. It takes 23 hours 56 minutes for each complete spin, almost a day and a night.

The Earth's crust

There are two kinds of crust: continental and oceanic. The crust of which the continents are made is called sial, because it contains a lot of silicon and aluminum. This crust is very old. Many parts of the continents are more than 1.5 billion years old. Continental crust is usually about 19 miles thick, but under high mountain ranges it extends down to 43 miles like roots pushing into the mantle below.

Beneath the sial is the sima. This kind of crust is denser than the sial and contains a lot of silicon and magnesium. The sima also forms the crust under the oceans, where it is less than 4 miles thick.

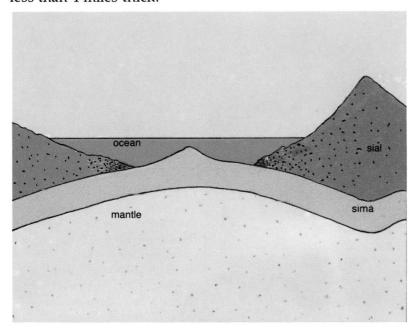

The Earth in its place

If you stand and watch the stars move around the sky at night, or follow the path of the Sun across the sky by day, it seems as if the Earth is the center of the universe. But the Earth is really only a very tiny part of the universe. It is a planet — a round ball of rock and gases that travels in its own special path around the Sun. Our Sun has at least nine planets, each traveling in its own path or "orbit."

The Earth is the third planet nearest to the Sun. It lies between Venus and Mars. The Sun and planets make up the solar system. The solar system is part of a galaxy — the Milky Way — a huge revolving mass of millions of solar systems. Scattered across the universe are billions of galaxies.

The hot core

Early miners found that as they went deeper, it got hotter. We now know that as you go deeper into the Earth, the temperature increases for some distance down by about 2°F for every 110 feet. The center of the Earth is probably about 10,800°F.

Inside the Earth there is enormous pressure due to gravity. You can feel the pressure of gravity if you put a pile of books on your head. The more books you add, the greater the pressure you feel.

Imagine the pressure of thousands of miles of rock. No wonder the rocks change shape.

---*Did you know?*---

The average circumference of the Earth is about 24,946 miles, and it weighs 6,590,000,000,000,000,000,000 tons.

The highest temperature ever recorded on land, in the shade, is 136°F, in the Libyan desert. The lowest is −127°F, at Vostok, in Antarctica.

More about the Earth's crust (pp.10, 11, 36); gravity (pp.104, 105, 106, 107); the solar system (pp.134 – 141)

A giant jigsaw puzzle

Crustal plates

Look at this map of the world's crustal plates. It also shows where some of the world's important volcanoes are found. What do you notice about the positions of the volcanoes in relation to the plates? (Answer on page 150). Can you see the volcanoes are arranged in a circle or ring? This is called the "Ring of Fire." Mountains are made where oceanic plates and continental plates move together. What would you expect to find where the Nazca Plate meets the South American Plate? Answer on page 150.

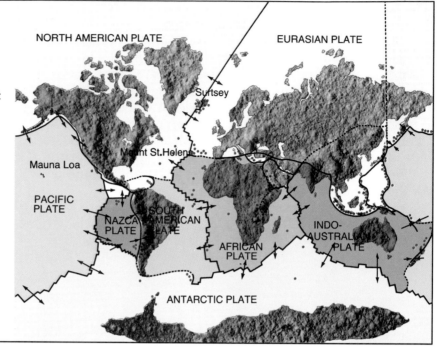

The Earth's surface

The crust is the solid surface of the Earth on which we live and work. It also forms the floor of the world's oceans and seas. The crust lies on top of another layer called the mantle. The mantle is very hot and scientists think that much of its rock is soft, like runny toffee. There are even hotter rocks deeper down below the mantle, nearer the Earth's core.

Gigantic plates

The Earth's crust isn't one continuous layer like the skin of an orange. Instead, it is made up of a number of gigantic pieces rather like a huge jigsaw puzzle. Each piece is called a crustal plate. Some of these plates form the floors of the oceans. Other plates carry the continents. The plates vary in thickness and density. Those forming the ocean floors are only about 3.7 miles thick and they are made of very dense materials. The plates carrying the continents are much thicker and lighter. In mountainous areas this part of the Earth's crust may be as thick as 43 miles. If you wanted to bore a hole through the Earth's crust to reach the mantle, which part of the Earth's surface would you choose to start digging? Answer on page 150.

Plates on the move

The molten rock around the Earth's core heats up the mantle above. Currents of molten rock rise up through the mantle like boiling water in a saucepan. As each current hits the underneath of the crustal plates, it starts to spread out. This slowly pushes or tears the crust apart. The plates are always on the move. Some are slowly being pulled apart. Others are slowly being pushed together. Some of them even collide with each other. These movements cause earthquakes and volcanic activity.

▲ Iles des Saintes, off the coast of Guadeloupe, are part of a chain of volcanic islands.

Island arcs and hot spots

Sometimes as two plates move toward each other on the ocean floor, one is forced down under the other. This forms a deep-sea trench. Here, molten rock breaks through the seabed and chains of volcanic islands are formed — a volcanic arc. Sometimes volcanic islands are formed when a plate passes over a hot spot on the ocean floor.

The spreading sea floor

Where two plates meet on the ocean floor, an oceanic ridge is formed. In these regions, molten rock from below the crust rises up through the joint between the plates. As the molten rock reaches the surface of the ocean floor, it spreads out and cools.

Subduction zone

An oceanic plate is heavier than a continental plate. When two plates like this meet, the heavier oceanic plate moves under the continental plate. This is called a subduction zone. Subduction zones are usually areas of mountains and volcanoes.

continent

spreading ridge

island arc

deep-sea trench

More about the sea floor (pp.70, 71); volcanoes (pp.16, 17)

11

The moving continents

▲ This photograph of the Earth was taken from 93,000 miles out in space. Which large continent can you see? Answer on page 150.

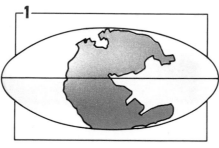

1

300 million years ago
If you could have looked at the Earth 300 million years ago it would have looked like this. The continents were all joined together into one super-continent called Pangaea.

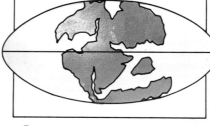

2

180 million years ago
About 180 million years ago, Pangaea began to break up into two smaller continents. The one in the north was called Laurasia, the one in the south Gondwana.

3

135 million years ago
About 135 million years ago, North America began to separate from Europe and Asia. Africa began to separate from South America. India began to drift north.

The changing Earth
Everyone is familiar with a map of the world and the shapes and positions of the continents. But the Earth hasn't always looked as it does today. About seventy years ago, a geologist called Alfred Wegener suggested that the continents were once found much closer together than they are today. He also suggested that they have moved into their present positions over many millions of years. The maps tell the story.

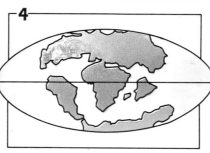

4

65 million years ago
About 65 million years ago, the continents had drifted farther apart. Can you recognize their different shapes? Note Australia is still joined to Antarctica.

5

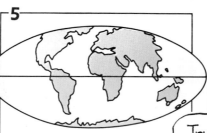

TODAY
This map shows the continents in their present positions. But remember, they are still drifting.

Try drawing a map to show what you think the world will look like 50 million years from now.

Evidence from the rocks

When you look at a present-day map of the world, it is easy to imagine how the continents once fitted much closer together. But is there any real evidence for this? Geologists have now studied the rocks from the east coast of South America and the west coast of Africa and have found them to be the same. They have the same structure and they are the same age. This suggests they were once part of the same piece of land. That was 200 million years ago.

Cetiosaurid

Evidence from birds

South America, Africa and Australia each has its own species of large, flightless bird. South America has the rhea, Africa the ostrich and Australia the emu and cassowary. All these birds look very similar. Why are such similar birds found so far apart and how did they get there? Remember, they can't fly! Perhaps the answer to this puzzle lies in a common ancestor which walked to all three continents when they were still joined together.

rhea
ostrich
emu

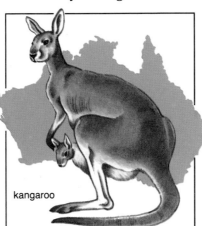
kangaroo

The pouched mammals of Australia first appeared in South America about 100 million years ago. They traveled to Australia by walking across the Antarctic. This was possible 100 million years ago because the continents were much closer together. Once the continents started to drift apart, the Australian marsupials became stranded. They could no longer move on to other parts of the world. Most of their relatives in South America were killed by other animals. And so, today, most of the world's surviving marsupials are in Australia.

Dinosaur puzzle

Fossil bones of dinosaurs called Cetiosaurids have been found in many different parts of the world. These were very big dinosaurs, some as long as 70 feet and weighing over 16 tons. How did they get to parts of the world as far afield as North America and Australia? They certainly pose a problem. Can you solve the dinosaur puzzle? Answer on page 150.

—Did you know?—

Every year, North America and Europe separate by an additional ¾ inch. In 50 million year's time they will have moved 620 miles farther apart.

Fossil ferns have been discovered in the Antarctic. It is likely that fossil dinosaurs will also be found there.

More about moving continents (pp.10, 11, 30 – 33); fossils (pp.30, 31, 32, 33)

The origin of rocks

Deep heat

All the rocks on Earth contain materials which were once inside the Earth's crust. Deep under the Earth's crust, the rock gets so hot that it melts to form what we call magma. This is because of the great pressure due to all the rocks above, which raises its temperature.

Rocks can also melt nearer the surface if there is a source of heat, such as where the ocean floor is dragged under the continents as they move. This generates heat by friction as the rocks rub together. Hot spots also occur where there is radioactivity in the crust.

What are rocks made of?

Rocks are complicated structures. They contain complex chemicals called minerals. Many of these are present as crystals — solid structures that have definite shapes with sharp, clear edges and corners.

▲ Surtsey, off Iceland, is one of the newest volcanoes in the world. It first erupted in 1963.

Although the Earth's crust seems very firm and solid, it is under great stresses and strains, and in places it is very weak. In these places, the magma wells up on to the surface as volcanoes or lava flows. As it cools, it becomes solid, forming new rock. Rocks which are formed directly by the cooling of magma are called igneous rocks.

Clues to the past

By studying the kinds of minerals in a rock and the size of the crystals, you can learn how the rock was formed. The chemical composition of the magma and its temperature affect how thick a liquid it is. Very hot, liquid magmas rise to the surface quickly and flow across the surface as lava. They cool rapidly, which gives crystals little time to form. So they have very small crystals. Thicker magmas, which flow slowly, like treacle, may cool slowly before they reach the surface. Large crystals have more time to form.

Obsidian is a volcanic rock that looks like black glass. It appears to have no crystals in it. How do you think it was formed? Answer on page 150.

▲ A thin section of hornblende, viewed by polarized light.

Rocks in close-up

When geologists (scientists who study rocks) want to look at small crystals, they first grind the rock until they have a piece thin enough to put under a microscope. When they shine a special light, called a polarized light, on the rock section, the crystals show up in beautiful colors.

▲ These rocks at the Giant's Causeway in Ireland are made of a volcanic rock called basalt. Millions of years ago, when the basalt cooled, it shrank and cracked to form thousands of regular, six-sided columns. They look like a huge staircase leading down to the sea.

More about crystals (pp. 120, 121); magma (pp. 16, 17)

Volcanoes

What makes volcanoes?

In places deep under the Earth's crust, the rocks have melted to form magma, or liquid rock. Sometimes the pressure of the rocks above is so great that where there is a line of weakness, such as a fault plane or fissure (crack) in the crust, the magma rises to the Earth's surface to form a volcano. As the magma nears the surface, the gases dissolved in it bubble up and escape. The molten rock without its gases is now called lava.

Building up the cone

Often the magma is prevented from reaching the surface by a layer of rock. Then the pressure builds up until it bursts through with a great explosion, sending ash, rock and molten lava high into the air. The large amount of gas mixed with the magma expands rapidly as the pressure is released, blasting away the overlying rock. Some volcanoes explode with the force of several nuclear bombs.

Once it has escaped into the cooler air, the lava solidifies to form rock. Rocks and solidified lava build up around the vent (the mouth of the funnel from which the lava is escaping) to form a cone. Often molten lava pours in red-hot rivers down the sides of the cone for some time after the initial eruption, covering the rocks that first formed the cone. The lava may solidify in the vent and block it, so that the volcano has frequent explosive eruptions. These add more layers of rock and lava to the cone, building it up higher and higher.

A big bang

In 1883, the volcanic island of Krakatoa in Indonesia erupted with such force that the explosion was heard over 3,000 miles away. As the magma chamber below emptied, much of the island fell into the crater. The disturbance caused a great tidal wave which swept over the coasts of Java and Sumatra, killing 36,000 people.

Dormant and extinct volcanoes

Many volcanoes erupt only occasionally, when enough pressure has built up to cause another explosion. Volcanoes which are not erupting at the moment, but which are still capable of erupting, are called dormant volcanoes. Some volcanoes remain dormant for thousands of years. Others erupt several times a year.

If it is no longer possible for a particular volcano to erupt, perhaps because the supply of hot magma has disappeared, it is said to be extinct. You can sometimes recognize extinct volcanoes by their shape, but soon the rocks are weathered away. Often the plug in the vent is made of harder rock than the surrounding area, and stands out as a pillar-like hill, like the one in the picture on the right.

▲ This church at Puy, in France, is built on top of a hill of hard lava. The whole hill is a volcanic plug left after the rest of the volcano has been weathered away.

◄ Crater Lake, Oregon, United States. When the top has been blown out of a volcanic cone by an eruption, it often leaves a crater called a caldera. Calderas are also made when the rubble forming the tip of the cone collapses into the vent.

Kicking up the dust

Some volcanoes send out vast quantities of ash, which spread through the atmosphere and can affect the weather for months afterwards. In 1982, the hot ash from Mount St. Helens destroyed over 58 square miles of forest. In the same year a cloud of dust from El Chichon in Mexico reached up to 20 miles into the atmosphere and encircled the Earth.

When Vesuvius, in Italy, erupted in A.D. 79, the poisonous gases given off suffocated people where they stood, and the town of Pompeii was buried in ash. Later it rained, and the rain turned the ash into a kind of cement which flowed down the mountain, and preserved forever the shapes of the dead people and animals.

Did you know?

Mauna Kea in Hawaii rises 31,000 feet from the bed of the ocean, 13,680 feet of it above sea level. It is the highest mountain in the world and contains 1,000 cubic miles of lava. Its base is over 60 miles across.

One of the newest volcanoes in the world is Surtsey, off Iceland, which erupted for the first time in 1963.

More about tidal waves (p.28); volcanoes (pp.27, 36)

Rocks from down under

The underground melting pot

In places deep in the Earth's crust and below, it is hot enough for rocks to melt. The gases trapped in the molten rock, which is called magma, force it up through the crust along the lines of weakness. As the magma rises through the cooler rocks above, it also cools, and sometimes becomes solid rock before it reaches the surface.

Millions of years later, this rock may become exposed at the surface, as the rocks above it are worn away by the wind, ice and water. Often it is much harder than the surrounding rocks, and stands out as ridges and hills.

All shapes and sizes

Sometimes the magma pushes up the rocks above to form huge chambers before it finally solidifies. These are called batholiths. Some of them are enormous. For example, one batholith in the United States is over 990 miles long and 150 miles wide.

Often the magma flows between the beds of sedimentary rocks. These rocks were formed by sand and mud deposited in ancient seas and lakes. They are usually made up of layers of rock separated by lines of weakness, called bedding planes. When the magma solidifies along a bedding plane, it is called a sill. Where it rises upward along a crack that crosses the bedding planes, it forms a dike. Sometimes the rocks above are pushed upward, so the magma forms a laccolith. Sometimes the rocks below are weak and sag to form a lopolith.

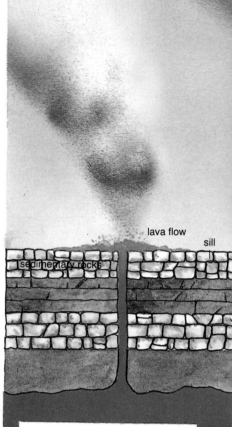

lava flow

sill

sedimentary rocks

▲ Mineral terraces shape the landscape of Yellowstone National Park, in the United States.

Hot water for free

Heat from magma can warm up underground water, producing hot springs and geysers. Often this hot water has risen from a great depth, dissolving minerals from the rocks on its way. When the water cools at the surface, the minerals are deposited as rock. Geysers are fountains of hot gas and water that explode from the ground at intervals. Old Faithful geyser, in the Yellowstone National Park in the United States, is named for the regular timing of its spurts, which can reach a height of over 220 feet.

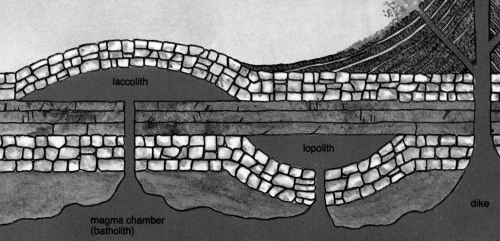

volcano

lava

ash

laccolith

lopolith

dike

magma chamber
(batholith)

Hidden treasures

As the magma cools, certain minerals solidify into crystals sooner than others. Often they sink down through the magma and become concentrated in thin layers. Many of our gemstones and metal ores are formed in this way. Precious crystals, such as diamond and amethyst, are found lining narrow cracks through which magma or hot, mineral-rich water once flowed.

▲ This dike is so hard that it forms a ridge above the surrounding rocks in the Sinai Desert.

Did you know?

A geyser in New Zealand holds the world record, reaching a height of 1,500 feet in 1904.

A lopolith near Lake Superior in the United States contains about 4,800 cubic miles of rock.

The Sierra Nevada batholith lies under 150,000 square miles of California.

If lava cools very fast, while its gases are still bubbling out, it forms spongy rock called pumice. Pumice is very light and will float on water.

19

More about crystals (pp. 120, 121); geysers (pp. 111, 115)

From sand to stone

The everchanging surface

The surface of the Earth is continually being worn away by wind, water, and ice. The broken-down rock is washed or blown into lakes or out to sea, where it settles on the bottom to form deep layers of sediment. Over millions of years, the weight of later sediments creates a great pressure, which helps to turn the old sediments into rock. Later still, the great stresses and strains that affect the Earth's crust may fold and crumple these new rocks and push them up to form new mountain ranges. These, in their turn, will be worn away.

▲ Sedimentary rocks in the Painted Desert, Arizona. Even the trees have been turned to rock by crystallizing minerals.

The giant layer cake

Most sedimentary rocks look as if they are made like a layer cake. You can see lots of bands of slightly different colors. These bands were originally laid down at different times, separated by a period when the sediments were worn down by wind or water. When new sediments were later laid down on top, the particles were of a different size or chemical makeup, so they look a different color. The rocks now split easily along the old bedding planes — the joins between the rock beds.

Natural cement

First, the sediments are squashed into a smaller space by the weight of more sediment piling on top of them.

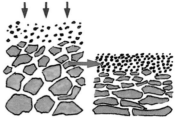

Water trickling through, deposits mineral crystals which gradually cement the fragments together.

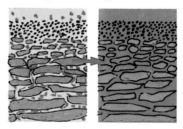

As the sediments become more and more deeply buried, the pressure increases, and they are also warmed by heat from deep in the Earth. This causes changes in the minerals, and the sediment becomes a solid mass of rock — a "sedimentary rock."

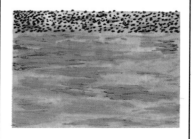

New rocks from old

Sediments come in many different shapes and sizes. Up in the mountains, frost breaks up the rocks into jagged fragments which tumble down the mountain and build up at the foot in piles, called screes. Upland stream beds are lined with large rounded boulders, while lowland rivers leave a trail of mud and silt. The sea produces its own toll of pebbles and sandy beaches, crumbling cliffs and growing sand dunes. Far out to sea, the finest particles of sand and mud finally sink to the ocean floor.

Different sediments form different kinds of rock. Rounded boulders and pebbles form solid masses called conglomerates, sharp-edged fragments become breccias, smaller particles become sandstones, and still finer particles develop into mudstones and clays.

▲ These rocks are mudstones. They were formed from tiny particles of clay millions of years ago. The rock beds are almost vertical. Why do you think this is? Answer on page 150.

Make your own sediments

Try digging up a narrow section of soil, about 12 inches deep. Put it in a tall jar of water and shake it up. Then allow the soil to settle. You will see that the largest pieces settle first. After several days, your jar will contain many layers of soil particles, with the heaviest at the bottom.

Settling down

Winds and rivers can carry small rock particles much farther than large ones. The large ones are deposited first, while the fine ones are carried out to sea.

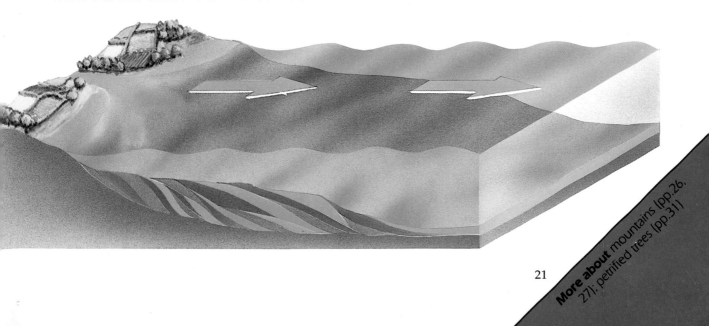

More about mountains (pp.26, 27); petrified trees (pp.31)

Salts, shells and sediments

Rocks that come from the sea

River water contains many minerals and salts dissolved from the rocks over which the water has passed. These collect in lakes and seas. If the water then evaporates in the Sun, they turn into crystals. The crystals settle to the bottom as sediments, called evaporites, and may later be turned into rock. Such rock is forming today in the Dead Sea, the Mediterranean Sea and around the Persian Gulf.

▲ Rocklike pillars of evaporites at Mono Lake, California.

Salt or sand?

In parts of the New Mexico desert, gypsum (calcium sulfate) forms when the hot, dry winds blow over shallow pools and lakes. The gypsum crystals are picked up by the desert winds and whipped up to form the white dunes of White Sands National Monument.

Cave rocks

In underground caves, the lime contained in the water that slowly drips from the roof, forms fascinating rock formations, called stalagmites and stalactites.

Rock plants?

On land, decaying plant material collects in bogs and swamps and is slowly changed, first to peat and then, after millions of years, to coal.

Animals can make rocks, too

Rock fragments are not the only kinds of sediments. Many animals extract salts from the surrounding water to make mineral skeletons and shells. When they die, they sink to the sea bed. Over thousands or even millions of years, these shells and skeletons become cemented together to form rocks of limestone or chalk.

▲ The surface waters of the oceans and lakes contain millions of microscopic floating plants and animals with tiny shells of lime or silica (a clear glasslike mineral).

▲ Mussels, clams, crabs, shrimps, sea urchins and starfish all produce rock-forming minerals.

—Did you know?—

Chalk is made up of shells so tiny that they can only be seen with a microscope.

Under the Mediterranean Sea, evaporite sediments are over 6,550 feet thick.

Limestones are forming today by evaporation in the shallow seas off coasts of southern Florida, the Bahamas and the Persian Gulf.

Fossil sea shells can be found in rocks thousands of feet up in the Andes of South America. These rocks were formed from sediments deposited in the sea, and later lifted high above sea level when mountains were formed.

▲ Fossil shells and corals make up a large part of this limestone.

More about limestone and caves (pp. 40, 41); peat and coal (pp. 112, 113, 129)

23

Rearranging the rocks

Rocks are not forever

In many parts of the world, layers of mud, sand and minerals are accumulating in seas, lakes and river basins. As more and more layers are deposited, the older ones are pushed deeper and deeper into the Earth as the crust sags under their weight. If they sink too deep into the Earth's crust, they can be changed again by the great heat there, and by the pressure of all the overlying rocks. These altered rocks, formed deep inside the Earth, are called metamorphic rocks. In Greek, "meta" means change, and "morph" means form.

▲ These sedimentary rocks have been changed by pressure into metamorphic rocks.

Baking the rocks

Deep in the crust, the sedimentary rocks may come into contact with hot molten magma. A large chamber of magma pushing into the rocks above can heat the rock to 1,300°F, and may take more than a million years to cool. Sometimes this takes place on a very large scale, affecting the rocks for miles around. Mineral-rich water, heated by magma from below, may pass over the rock, dissolving some of its minerals and depositing others in their place. As the rock bakes, some minerals change shape, while others break down and react with each other to form new minerals. It can become difficult to see where the old layers once were.

From mud to gneiss

When mud is deposited in great thicknesses, it forms clay as water is forced out of the sediments and the mud particles stick together. As the clay is laid down, its flaky mineral crystals lie parallel to the surface, and the pressure of the overlying sediments eventually turns them into shale.

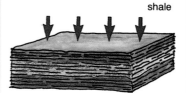

shale

Under great pressure, due to Earth movements, the flaky minerals recrystallize in a new direction to form slate.

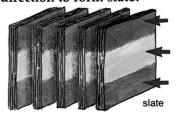

slate

Still greater pressure and heat turns the slate into gneiss. The old mineral layers are twisted and squeezed into new patterns.

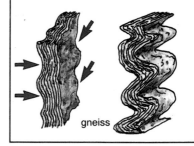

gneiss

▼ Marble is a metamorphic rock formed from limestone. It is difficult to imagine where the original rock layers were.

Do-it-yourself mountain building

Rocks are not as rigid as they may appear. If they are put under enough pressure, they become slightly plastic. Sometimes the forces at work in the Earth's crust press on the rocks, thrusting them up into folds and forming mountain ranges.

Take several different colored pieces of cloth and lay them on top of each other. These represent the layers of your rock. Now place a book on each end and push. See how the cloth folds.

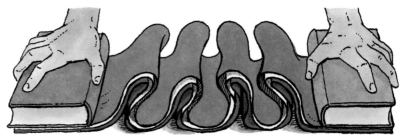

Do-it-yourself metamorphosis

If the pressure is very great, the rocks become even more plastic. Try making your rock layers of modeling clay instead of cloth. You may have to use your fingers to make the folds. Now try pressing down on one end. What do you see? Now try pushing from one side. What happens to the colored bands? What happens if you warm the clay first? Does it change shape and color more easily? You can find the answers on page 150.

Faults

Rocks do not always bend under pressure. Sometimes they break along lines of weakness, and blocks of rock slip past each other. These fractures along which the rocks move are called faults.

Precious stones

Some of the minerals that form under high temperatures or pressures are precious stones. Rubies, sapphires and spinels are formed when molten magma comes into contact with limestone. Garnets and emeralds, often found in metamorphic rocks, are the result of great pressures inside the Earth's crust.

More about faults (p. 27); making mountains (pp. 26, 27)

Making mountains

What goes up, comes down

If you look down at the ground you are standing on, most likely your feet rest on a layer of soil, the broken remains of larger rocks. The rubble that forms mountain screes, the boulders that line the beds of streams and rivers, and the pebbles and sand that form our beaches, are all broken-down rocks. These gradually wear away to smaller and smaller pieces until they come to lie at the bottom of some lake or sea.

If the Earth's surface has been wearing away like this for some 4.6 billion years, you might expect it to have been reduced to a flat, featureless plain by now. Far from it. There are still mighty mountain ranges in many parts of the world. This is because new mountains are still being made.

▲ Folded rocks exposed on the English coast.

In some places you can see huge folds of rock, evidence of the great upheavals which affect the Earth's crust and force up the rocks to form mountains. Mountain ranges thousands of miles long, like the Alps, the Rockies, the Andes and the Himalayas, can be formed by folding. The highest land mountain in the world, Mount Everest, now 29,028 feet above sea level, is made up of sedimentary rocks that were formed in the sea that once separated India from Asia.

Fold mountains

Sedimentary rocks are formed from the broken-down remains of older rocks, which collect on the sea floor. These are eventually turned into solid rock masses.

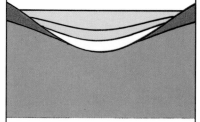

Vast thicknesses of rock accumulate as the Earth's crust sags under the weight.

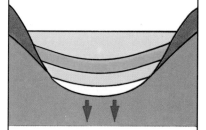

Great pressures then compress the layers of sediment until they rise up in folds to form new land.

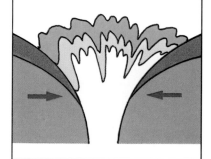

Block mountains

Sometimes the rocks give way under the strain, and split along lines of weakness called faults. Whole blocks of rock may be tilted, or even lifted up above the surrounding rocks. They form mountain blocks which rise abruptly from the plains around them. The great Sierra Nevada mountains, in the western United States, were formed in this way.

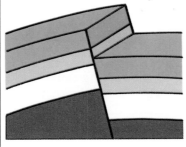

Great flat-bottomed valleys are formed by faulting, too. They are called rift valleys. One such valley runs north-ward from Central Africa to the Red Sea.

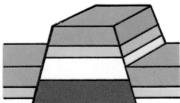

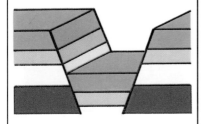

▲ Faults in the ground have caused the land to slip sideways in this garlic field in California. This is due to the great stresses and strains in the Earth's crust in this area. You can see where the furrows no longer line up.

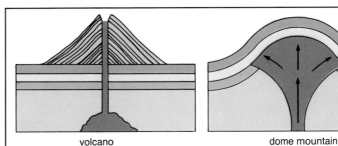

volcano   dome mountain

Volcanic mountains

Active volcanoes are also growing mountains. Molten rock from deep inside the Earth is forced on to the surface to form characteristic cone-shaped hills.

Sometimes the rocks are strong enough to resist the pressure of the rising magma, or molten rock, below. They are simply bent into a dome, forming a rounded mountain. In time, these rocks are worn away, and the hard volcanic rock forms the mountain.

More about volcanoes (pp.16, 17); looking at rocks (pp.34, 35)

Earthquakes

LISABONA

Source of the trouble

The exact point where the rocks start to move and cause the earthquake is called the focus (F). The point on the surface immediately above the focus is the epicenter (E).

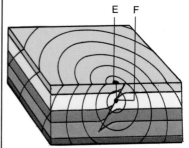
E   F

The curving lines link points receiving equal shocks.

Earthquakes can be devastating natural events. The ground shakes, buildings collapse, fires start, and giant waves pour over the coasts and sweep inland. Earthquakes are signs of the great stresses and strains which affect the Earth's crust. Rocks which are being compressed or stretched suddenly give way and crack and slip along what is called a fault. This sets up vibrations which travel hundreds of miles through the crust and even through the Earth's core.

Quakeproof buildings

In areas which often experience earthquakes, tall buildings are built on concrete "rafts" that literally float on the Earth's crust as the earthquake waves pass. Streets can be made wider to reduce injury from falling buildings.

Tsunamis

Tsunamis are giant tidal waves that are set up by earthquakes which affect the ocean floor. When out to sea, the waves crests may be over 100 miles apart and only a few feet high. But as they reach shallow water, they slow down and the wave height increases dramatically, sometimes reaching heights of 50 to 100 feet. As a tsunami approaches the coast, the sea draws away from the shore, often exposing the sea bed itself. Then it rushes back as giant waves. A tsunami can travel at 500 mph. It can cross the ocean and affect coasts thousands of miles away from the site of the original earthquake.

Using earthquakes to study the Earth

Scientists can measure the vibrations of earthquakes using an instrument called a seismograph. The movements are traced with a pen on a revolving drum of paper.

Scientists have discovered that there are three kinds of vibrations, which travel like waves — seismic waves — through the Earth's crust. P waves travel right through the Earth's molten core, while S waves can travel only through solid parts of the crust and mantle. Ground waves travel along the surface and can cause a lot of damage.

P waves travel fastest, so they reach the seismograph first. The time between the arrival of the P and S waves tells scientists how far away the epicenter of the earthquake is. These measurements also tell us about the inside of the Earth, since different rocks bend the seismic waves to different degrees.

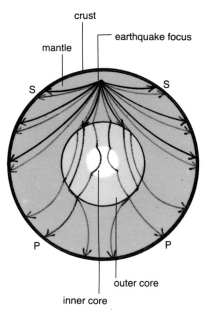

▲ Earthquake disaster in Anchorage, Alaska, in 1964. This street sank about 25 feet during the earthquake.

Predicting earthquakes

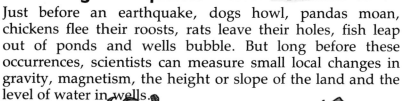

Just before an earthquake, dogs howl, pandas moan, chickens flee their roosts, rats leave their holes, fish leap out of ponds and wells bubble. But long before these occurrences, scientists can measure small local changes in gravity, magnetism, the height or slope of the land and the level of water in wells.

—Did you know?—

Over a million earthquakes occur every year. Most are so small that no one notices them.

In 1812, tremors in Missouri in the United States changed the course of the Mississippi River.

The Alaskan earthquake of 1964 was one of the largest this century, releasing energy equivalent to 12,000 atomic bombs. During this earthquake, one six-story building was carried almost 10 feet sideways, undamaged.

One of the strongest earthquakes in history occurred in China in 1556, killing over 800,000 people.

More about faults (pp.25, 27); seismographs (p.99)

The story of fossils

Reading the Earth's "pages"

To a geologist, the Earth's rocks are like the pages of a history book. They tell the geologist a story. However, the Earth's story is more difficult to read than a book. Rocks are often broken. Some are bent and others are upside down. Sometimes rocks are scattered over a wide area and some are missing altogether. Imagine trying to read a story where some of the pages are missing! The clues to the Earth's story lie in the fossils the rocks contain.

What is a fossil?

Fossils are the remains or traces of animals and plants. The remains are usually preserved in rocks, but other kinds of fossils have been found. Many fossils are millions of years old. When an animal or plant dies, its body is either eaten by animals or it decays. However, hard parts such as teeth, bones and shells are often preserved. They become fossilized. Many fossils are the remains of sea creatures. This is because many of the Earth's rocks were formed under the sea.

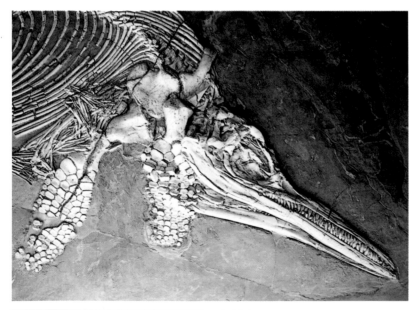

Miss Anning as a child ne'er passed
A pin upon the ground
But picked it up and so at last
An Ichthyosaurus found.'

▲ This is a fossil of an ichthyosaur. The first ichthyosaur was found in 1810 by an 11-year-old girl called Mary Anning.

How a fossil is formed

A sea-living animal dies and sinks to the sea bed.

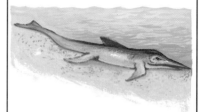

The soft body slowly decays. Its skeleton becomes covered in layers of mud which gradually settle and become solid rock.

At a much later date movements of the Earth buckle the sea bed and it rises above sea level.

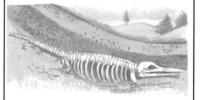

Erosion removes the rocks covering the fossil and it is now exposed on land.

Moulds and casts

The buried remains of animals and plants usually change. Shells and skeletons are turned into stone. Geologists say they become petrified. Plant remains including tree trunks are also turned to stone. As water filters through the rock it gradually dissolves the dead animal or plant remains. Sometimes the dead body is not replaced after it has decayed. If this happens a hollow is left in the rock. This is called a mould fossil. If the space in the rock is filled up with mineral salts dissolved in the water, a fossil, called a cast fossil, is produced. This type of fossil is formed in the same way as a jelly is formed when it is poured into a mould.

▲ This is a mould fossil of a dinosaur bone. The dinosaur lived about 150 million years ago. In this case the bone was dissolved and then not replaced. An impression of the bone is left long after the bone itself disappeared.

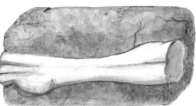

▲ This is a cast fossil of a dinosaur bone. This kind of fossil was formed when the bone of the dead dinosaur was dissolved by water and then the empty space was filled with mineral salts. The space became stone.

▲ This is a fossil of a trilobite. Trilobites lived 600 million years ago. Is this a picture of a mould fossil or cast fossil? Answer on page 150.

Making a pine cast fossil

Press a pine cone into a piece of flat modeling clay and then remove it.

Fill the depression left by the cone with liquid plaster of Paris or modeling wax.

When the plaster of Paris or modeling wax has hardened, remove the modeling clay. What is left is the cast fossil of the cone.

Did you know?

Fossil dinosaur footprints have been found in North America. They were left in soft mud more than 100 million years ago. Scientists have also found fossilized dinosaur eggs and even dinosaur droppings!

More about trilobites (p.35); sedimentary rock (pp.20, 21)

What fossils tell us

Where to look for fossils

You can sometimes find fossils in fields or even in your garden. However, it is much better to look for fossils in freshly exposed rocks. Look in quarries and around the base of sea cliffs. Even piles of clay dug up on building sites and roadworks are worth looking at.

But remember! Always ask permission before you start searching, and take care to protect yourself.

Remember! Always look in sedimentary rocks like limestone or shale.

Tools for hunting

All you need is a geologist's hammer and a chisel. Fossils need to be chipped away very carefully. You will also need some cotton wool and some boxes to keep your fossils in. The cotton wool will protect more delicate fossils from becoming damaged. A small chest of drawers is also useful as a fossil cabinet in which to store your collection.

THE EARTH'S HISTORY

Layers of the past

Sedimentary rocks are formed in layers, one on top of the other. Think about an undisturbed region of sedimentary rocks. The oldest will be at the bottom and the rocks formed most recently at the surface. Fossils from the different layers are not exactly the same. Fossils show how animals and plants have changed over the past 600 million years. Each rock layer has its own characteristic fossil animals and plants. When a geologist finds the same kinds of fossils in rocks in different areas, he can say that the rocks are the same age. They were laid down at the same time. This kind of information helps geologists piece together the Earth's long history.

GEOLOGIST'S NOTEBOOK

Geological Periods	Plant and animal forms
Quaternary Period began 2 – 3 million years ago.	Last Ice Age. Arrival of Man.
Tertiary Period began 70 million years ago.	Modern mammals appear. The Age of Mammals.
Cretaceous Period began 135 million years ago.	Dinosaurs decline. Mammals increase. First flowering plants appear.
Jurassic Period began 180 million years ago.	Dinosaurs abundant. First birds appear.
Triassic Period began 225 million years ago.	Early dinosaurs. First mammals appear.
Permian Period began 270 million years ago.	Reptiles increase.
Carboniferous Period began 350 million years ago.	Age of Amphibians. First reptiles appear.
Devonian Period began 400 million years ago.	Age of Fishes. First amphibians appear.
Silurian Period began 450 million years ago.	Earliest land plants appear.
Ordovician Period began 500 million years ago.	First fish appear.
Cambrian Period began 600 million years ago.	First fossils, all of them invertebrates.

The Earth probably began 4.6 billion years ago

► This fossil leaf lived nearly 300 million years ago. The original leaf was squashed by layers of silt settling on top of it. The enormous weight compressed the leaf into a thin film of carbon. This shows up the outline of the leaf's surface pattern.

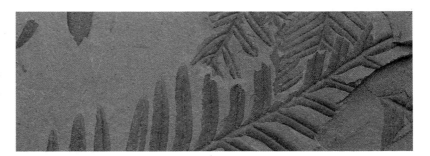

◄ Sometimes the whole body of an animal is preserved. This baby mammoth was found frozen in ice in Siberia in Russia. Frozen mammoths have also been found in Alaska. These animals probably fell into crevasses accidentally. They froze quickly so that all the body parts were perfectly preserved. Even the food in their stomachs was still fresh when the fossils were found.

Bogs and tar pits

Sometimes animals became trapped in bogs and tar pits. Pits near Los Angeles in California have been explored. They contain fossils in large numbers. Here scientists have found fossil sabre-toothed tigers and giant vultures with a wingspan of over 9 feet.

► These insects were fossilized in a drop of resin from a conifer tree 100 million years ago. As the resin hardened into amber, it preserved the insects.

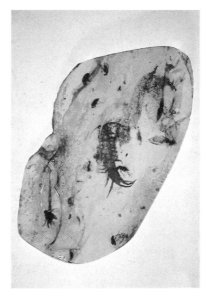

Fossil time clocks

All living things contain a certain amount of radio-active carbon, called carbon-14. This begins to break down after an animal or plant dies. Scientists have worked out how quickly carbon-14 breaks down. They measure the amount of carbon-14 still present in a fossil. This tells them how old the fossil is.

More about fossils (pp.30, 31, 34, 35, 36, 66); fossil clocks (pp.35, 133); carbon-14 (pp.133)

Reading the rocks

History on view

There are many places where you can look at rocks. The seashore, cliffs, quarries and road cuttings all reveal the patterns of the rocks.

How old is the Earth?

The Earth is at least 4.6 billion years old. Scientists know this from studying certain radioactive rocks in the Earth's crust. For most of its history, the Earth has been an empty, barren place. Plant and animal life began to appear less than 600 million years ago. From that time on, fossils in the rocks give us much more information about the state of the Earth.

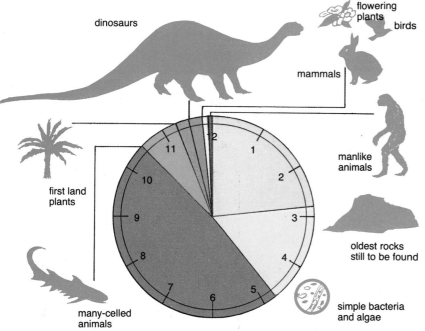

If you squeeze 4.6 billion years of Earth's history into the twelve hours of a clock face, the oldest rocks still to be found today were formed at about 2:52. Life first appeared in the form of simple bacteria and algae around 4:20. There was very little development then until around 10:30, when many-celled animals began to dominate the scene. At about 11:18 the first land plants appeared, and by 11:25, dinosaurs were roaming the land. Twenty-five minutes later, the birds and mammals had replaced the dinosaurs, and around the same time the first flowering plants appeared. Manlike animals arrived at only half a minute before noon. The entire history of civilization spans just the last tenth of a second.

Ancient climates

Rocks are a record of climate and the changing positions of land and sea. Limestone rocks are formed in warm, shallow seas. Coal is formed in coastal swamps. River sediments form sandstones, then shales as they get closer to the sea and smaller rock particles are dropped. Red sandstones are formed in hot, dry deserts.

Tracking ancient winds

Over millions of years, wind-blown sands are changed into sandstone rocks. The layers of sand that formed the original dunes are preserved in the rocks. From the angle and direction of these layers, we can tell the way the wind was blowing millions of years ago. The sizes of the grains in each layer tell us how strongly the wind was blowing.

Tracing ancient rivers

Sandstones formed from river sediments can tell us about the rate and direction of river flow, and the type of rocks through which the river flowed. The minerals in them tell us about the rocks. The river drops large boulders and pebbles high up in the mountains. But by the time it is wandering over its flood plain near the coast, it drops sand and eventually mud.

Rock around the clock

Fossils tell us about the age of rocks, as well as about past climates. Fossils are the remains of animals and plants that lived long ago. Just as today, certain animals and plants are found in certain places, so it was then. A particular kind or species of fossil lived only in a special place — a river, the sea, a mountain, a desert, etc., and a special climate. If the river dried up or the climate changed, the creature had to change too, in order to survive. If it did not change, it died out. So a particular species of fossil lived for only a short time (in geological terms this can mean millions of years). Where we find rocks containing similar fossils, we know they must have been formed at the same time.

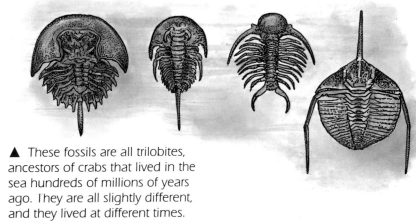

▲ These fossils are all trilobites, ancestors of crabs that lived in the sea hundreds of millions of years ago. They are all slightly different, and they lived at different times.

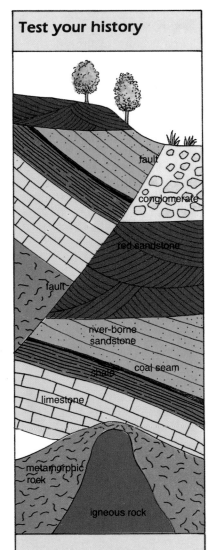

Test your history

fault

conglomerate

red sandstone

fault

river-borne sandstone

shale   *coal seam*

limestone

metamorphic rock

igneous rock

Look at the sequence of rocks above. Can you trace what has happened to the climate in this area since the time the bottom rocks were formed? Can you make any guesses about where the coast was in the past?

You can find out if you were right by looking up the answer on page 150.

▲ The rocks at the bottom of this picture were folded, tilted, then worn down. Later on, new sediments were laid down horizontally on top of them to form the upper layer of rock.

More about wind-blown sand (pp.52, 53, 55); river sediments (pp.44, 45)

35

Floating continents and underwater mountains

Colliding continents

The Earth's crust is made up of giant plates of rock which "float" on less dense rocks below. Movements of the semimolten rock below the crust cause these plates to drift slowly across the globe. Mountains are being made today where these great plates are colliding with each other. As the continents drift closer together, the sediments laid down in the seas that once separated them are folded and faulted into great mountains. The Alps are forming where the African plate is pushing up against the Eurasian plate, and the Himalayas where the Indian plate is being forced under the Eurasian plate.

▼ The highest mountain in the world, Mount Everest, now 29,028 feet above sea level, is made up of sedimentary rocks that were formed in the sea that once separated India from Asia.

The Ring of Fire

Mountain building produces great stresses and strains, which cause the surface rocks to fault and the deeper rocks to melt, causing earthquakes and volcanoes. Around the Pacific Ocean, the crustal plate that forms the floor of the ocean is forcing its way under the edges of the surrounding continents. Many earthquakes and volcanoes are asociated with this upheaval and form a "ring of fire" around the Pacific. Along the west coast of North and South America, the edges of the continents are crumpling to form the Rockies and the Andes. As the ocean floor is forced deeper under the surrounding continents, its rocks melt and give rise to volcanoes such as Mount St. Helens and the chains of volcanoes that form many of the peaks of the Andes.

Mountains under the sea

Running across the floors of the oceans are vast ranges of mountains called the mid-oceanic ridges. Some mountains rise thousands of feet from the ocean floor, and all are made of volcanic rocks. Along this line, molten rock, or magma, is forced up to the surface, where it forms lava flows and volcanoes. All along the ridge, new crust is being formed in this way. In places like Iceland, the mountains break the surface to form islands and island volcanoes.

▲ Where lava bubbles up deep under the ocean, it solidifes quickly to form these "pillow lavas."

The floating mountains

If you try floating a block of wood in a dish of water, you will see that a proportion of the wood remains below the water. If you add a weight to the top of the block, the amount of wood under the water increases. If you take the weight away, the block bobs up to its original position.

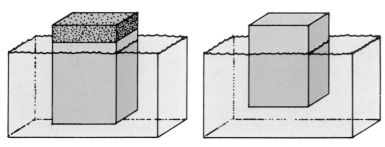

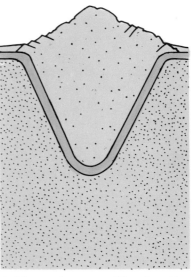

The same thing happens with mountain ranges. The weight of the mountains creates so much pressure that the rocks deep down in the Earth below become less solid, rather like runny toffee. Very high mountain ranges have "roots" of rock pushing deep into the semisolid rocks below. As the mountains are worn away, they "float" up to compensate, so exposing more rock at the surface to be worn away. This rising and sinking of the land is called isostasy.

▲ Mountain ranges "float" on the less dense rocks below.

▲ The deep valleys and gullies show how fast the Andes are being worn away. Yet they continue to rise to make up for it.

— Did you know? —

The highest point of land is Mount Everest, 29,028 feet above sea level. The lowest, the Dead Sea, is 1,286 feet below sea level. It lies in a rift valley.

The mid-oceanic ridge system is the longest mountain chain in the world. It crosses all the oceans, and is over 37,000 miles long.

The mountains of the mid-oceanic ridges occupy 38 million square miles. If they were not there, the sea level would be 800 feet lower.

More about crustal plates (pp.10, 11); the Ring of Fire (p.10)

37

Water can move mountains

The crumbling rocks

Mountains do not last forever. The deep valleys and gorges in our mountain ranges, and even the soil beneath our feet, are evidence that all the time rocks are being broken down and washed away. Wind, water and ice help in this process.

Clints and grikes

Limestone is particularly easily dissolved by the acids in rainwater. Limestone rocks have many vertical cracks, called joints, down which rainwater trickles. Water can also spread sideways along the bedding planes. The joints gradually become widened as the rock dissolves away, forming grikes. The limestone becomes divided up by the grikes into blocks, called clints. Because the water that falls on the limestone can run away down the grikes, limestone areas are often dry, even where there is plenty of rain.

▲ A limestone pavement clearly showing clints and grikes, in Yorkshire, England.

Dry valleys

Limestone areas have many dry valleys with no rivers in them. The rivers flowed thousands of years ago during the last ice age, when the rock was frozen and the rivers could not run away down the cracks in the rocks. Today, they flow deep underground in vast systems of caves and tunnels. This sort of country is called karst.

Pillars of earth

Where there is little plant cover to protect the soil, heavy rain washes it away very easily. These earth pillars were formed because large stones on the surface protected the earth below.

Dissolving rocks

If you stir salt, which is really crystals of sodium chloride, into a glass of water, the crystals disappear and the water has a salty taste. The salt is still there, but it is in solution — it has dissolved. Rocks are made up of minerals, and some of them simply dissolve in rainwater. Tiny gaps between the crystals in the rock allow the rainwater to trickle down, dissolving it away. The parts of the rock which do not dissolve are left as a crumbly mass, which is either washed away by the water, or remains to form the basis of soil.

The power of ice

When water freezes, it expands as it forms ice. As water in cracks in the rock freezes, it exerts a pressure of almost a ton per square inch on the surrounding rock as it expands. This shatters the rocks, and pieces break off and fall to the ground. In mountain regions, where the temperature falls below freezing at night, the broken rock fragments form piles, called screes, at the foot of the cliffs.

Rock-splitting trees

Tree roots are powerful in pushing through the soil. They reach into cracks in the rocks and expand, forcing the rock apart. Tree roots can split massive boulders. Even the roots of small weeds can push through roads and paths, breaking up the surface. How do they do it? Answer on page 150.

▲ Screes pile up at the foot of mountain peaks.

Acid rain

Rainwater is an acid. Carbon dioxide gas from the atmosphere and from the soil dissolves in the rainwater to form weak carbonic acid. The acid reacts chemically with some of the minerals in the rock, breaking them down and dissolving them. In places the rock may be rotted to a depth of 100 feet below the surface.

Industrial areas other gases, such as sulfur dioxide, also form acids with rain. You can see their effects on rock by the way stone statues crumble away.

—Did you know?—

The Karst region of Yugoslavia has some of the highest rainfall in Europe, about 94 inches a year, yet it has only one river. Why do you think this is? Answer on page 150.

Earthworms help to erode mountains. They bring fine, broken-down pieces of rock to the surface of the soil, where they can be washed away by the rain. Their burrows help air and rainwater to reach the rocks below and break them down.

More about limestone caves [pp. 40, 41]; solutions and dissolving [pp. 126, 127]

Caves

Underground worlds

Cave systems are some of the last unexplored parts of the Earth's crust. Caves are found in most kinds of rock, but by far the largest and most extensive cave systems are found in limestone.

Water gets into rocks in two ways. It can seep between the grains of rock, creeping downward. If you dig deep enough into the rocks, you will reach a level where they are full of water. This level is called the water table.

Water also trickles down cracks in the rocks, either along bedding planes where they slope downward, or down vertical joints. The rainwater dissolves some of the limestone as it goes, gradually widening the joints until they form deep swallowholes, or sinkholes. In places they are widened so much that caves are formed. Sometimes the cave roof collapses and an even larger cave, called a cavern, is formed. Some caverns are large enough to contain waterfalls and lakes.

The water flows on down until it reaches the water table. Where the water table reaches the surface, the underground water escapes as a river or spring.

Sea caves

The pounding of the sea against the cliffs soon breaks up the rocks along any lines of weakness. Caves are sometimes formed in this way. As the waves rush against the rock, they trap air in the small cracks already present. This compressed air also helps to attack the rocks. Sometimes the roofs of these caves collapse, and during storms plumes of sea spray spout out of their tops. You can stand on the cliffs and listen to the sea booming in the hollow beneath your feet.

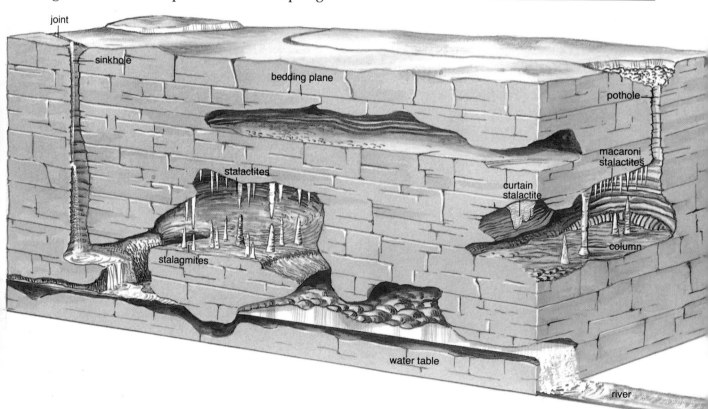

▲ Carlsbad Caverns in New Mexico are famous for their spectacular stalactites and stalagmites.

Stalactites and stalagmites

When the underground water evaporates, the lime dissolved in it is left behind, forming a rock called flowstone. Where water drips from the roof of a cave, it forms a long, hanging column called a stalactite. Where it splashes on the floor, it forms a fat tapering stump called a stalagmite. Sometimes stalactites and stalagmites join up to form columns. Stalactites can take 4,000 years to grow 1 inch, so big ones must be very old indeed.

Water trickling through cracks in the roof and walls forms hanging curtains of flowstone. Many other strange and wonderful shapes are formed by the dripping water. Pure limestone is transparent or white, but flowstones are usually colored yellowish or brown by impurities.

Ice caves

Tunnels and caves full of icicles sometimes form in glaciers. This happens when the ice pulls apart as it goes round a bend in the valley, or where rivers flowing along the bed of the glacier melt the ice.

Lava caves

When volcanoes erupt, they send streams of red-hot lava down the mountainside. The surface of the lava cools first and soon becomes solid. This solid roof protects the lava inside from contact with the cooler air, so it keeps on flowing. When the flowing, hot lava finally drains away, it leaves behind a long tunnel or lava tube.

Caves of history

For thousands of years, caves have provided shelter for humans and animals. The bones of animals that fell down sinkholes or crept into caves to die, and the tools, hearths, bones and cave paintings left behind by prehistoric man, tell us a lot about their life. One cave system in Austria contains the remains of 30,000 cave bears, a species now extinct.

— Did you know? —

The longest known stalactite is 194 feet long, in the Cueva de Nerja in Spain.

The tallest known stalagmite is 95 feet high, in Aven Armand Cave in France.

More about limestone (pp.38, 126); potholes (p.43)

Rivers shape the land

The power of water

Rivers and glaciers have shaped the landscape for millions of years. They have fashioned mountain ranges into hills and valleys, cut canyons and waterfalls, and carried vast quantities of sand, silt and mud into lakes and seas.

Water has enormous power to wear away rocks. One cubic yard of water weighs almost 1,700 pound. One inch of rainfall descending 1,640 feet, and draining about 0.4 square mile of hills, has stored energy equivalent to 44,000 tons of TNT, or two Hiroshima-sized nuclear bombs.

▲ Niagara Falls, on the Canada-United States border, is slowly retreating by about three feet a year. Eventually, the Falls will reach back and link together Lake Erie and Lake Ontario.

Rivers at work

River water breaks up the rocks by pounding them. When water flows fast, it gets turbulent — it swirls around in eddies and tumbles into hollows, putting great pressures on the rocks below.

The water picks up small rock particles from the rocks as they are broken down. Some minerals dissolve in the water; others are carried in suspension, held up by the water. The faster the flow, the larger the particles that can be carried. Fast-flowing water can even carry large boulders, sometimes weighing several tons. These roll or bounce along the riverbed. All these loads rub against the riverbeds and banks, breaking them up.

Where do rivers come from?

River water comes from rain or snow falling on the land. Water from melting glaciers and ice sheets runs away in streams and rivers. Rainwater may soak into the rocks and emerge farther down as springs. If the ground is already soaked, the water runs off downhill, following the path of the steepest slope. It collects in little gullies and hollows. Then the trickles join up to form streams and rivers.

Waterfalls

Different kinds of rock wear down at different rates. Hard rocks are worn down more slowly than soft rocks. Where a river flows over first a hard band of rock, then a soft band, it forms a ledge and creates a waterfall. As the softer rock is worn away, the water has to fall farther, and pounds the rocks below harder, so they wear away even faster. Often a deep pool develops at the base of the waterfall, where stones and boulders plunge into the water.

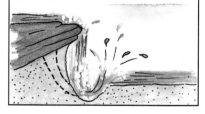

Valleys broad and narrow

The steeper the slope down which a river flows, the faster it flows, and the harder it cuts down into the rocks. Most rivers have steep gradients in their upper reaches, up in the hills. Here, they cut deep V-shaped valleys, or gorges.

Rivers on less steep ground have more curvy courses. Instead of rushing clean over obstacles, they flow round them. When water flows round a bend, the water on the outside of the bend has to flow farther than the water on the inside, so it flows faster. This cuts away the rock and helps to widen the valley.

Many rivers have very wide, flat valleys as they near the sea. When water flows more slowly, it drops some of its load of sand and mud. This builds up on the valley floor, and further reduces the slope of the ground.

▲ Potholes are formed when pebbles are swirled around in small hollows. The hollows get deeper, and the water swirls harder.

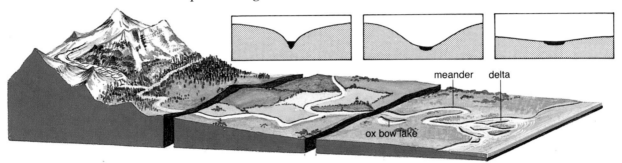

meander   delta

ox bow lake

Rising land and falling rivers

In some parts of the world the land is rising relative to the sea, or the sea level is falling. When this happens, the gradient of the river increases, and it cuts down faster into its bed. This can have spectacular results. The Grand Canyon has been formed over 10 million years, as the Colorado River has cut down about one mile through rising mountains. The shape of the canyon sides is due to bands of hard and soft rocks which wear away at different rates.

43

More about water (pp.122, 123); waterfalls (p.94)

Lazy rivers

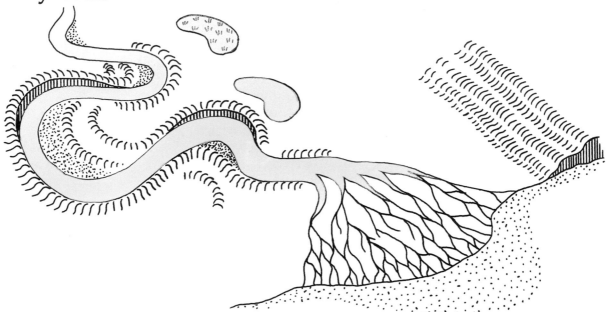

The flood plain

Many rivers have wide, almost flat, plains across which they flow to the sea. Here, the slope of the riverbed is very gentle, so the water flows slowly, swinging around obstacles in great curves, called meanders. As the river flows around a bend, the water on the outside of the bend has to flow farther than the water on the inside, so it flows faster, cutting into the banks and forming small cliffs. These cliffs gradually retreat as they are undermined by the fast-flowing water. On the inside of the bend the water flows more slowly, dropping its load and gradually forming sandbanks, which push the river farther and farther out in the curve.

The meanders slowly change course over the years, cutting a wide valley and depositing sediments over a vast area. These sediments are rich in minerals brought from the hills far away, and are often very fertile farm land.

Muddy waters
As it wears away its banks and bed, a river picks up a load of sediment — broken-down rock particles of various sizes, sand and silt. Fast-flowing rivers can carry larger particles than slow-flowing ones.

REMEMBER
When a river slows down, it drops the large particles first, then the finer ones.

Ox bow lakes
Sometimes a meander develops such a curve that the banks on one side are cut back into the banks on the other side. The river finds a shortcut, and the old meander is left as a semicircular lake.

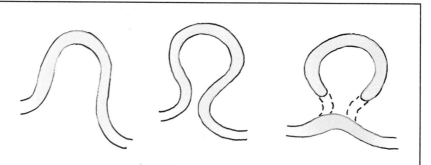

Deltas

When a river leaves its steep mountain valley and enters the more gently sloping lowlands, it slows down, shedding some of its load to form fan-shaped cones of sediment, called alluvial fans.

Deltas develop at some river mouths, building great banks of sediments far out into the sea. The river wanders across the almost flat delta, winding around every tiny pile of sediment, and breaking up into many strands of flowing water. Deltas also form where rivers enter the still water of a lake.

Building up the banks

When a river floods, it slows down as it flows over the flat land on either side. Much of its sediment is soon dropped to form raised banks called levees.

Floods

Heavy rain in the upper part of the river can cause floods on the river plain. A large river may be supplied by water draining from an area of thousands of square miles. This is called its catchment area. Even a small amount of rain, over a very large catchment area, can cause a great rise in the river level when funneled into the main river channel. In a large flood, a river may be ten times deeper and carry a hundred times more water than usual.

◀ The Amazon River flows into the South Atlantic Ocean at a rate of 6.2 million cubic feet a second. It drains an area of 2.3 million square miles.

─── *Did you know?* ───

The Yangtze River carries 1.8 billion tons of silt a year, enough to encircle the globe 27 times with an earthen bank over 3 feet high and 3 feet thick.

45

More about rivers (pp.42, 43); sediments (pp.20, 21)

Rivers of ice

A land under ice

About 6 million square miles of the Earth's surface are covered by permanent glaciers. Large expanses of ice form when more snow falls in winter than is melted in summer. This happens at the poles, and on the summits of high mountains. The continent of Antarctica is covered in an ice sheet one and a half times the size of the United States, containing around 600,000 cubic miles of ice. Yet the annual snowfall there is less than the annual rainfall of most deserts.

The average annual temperature at the South Pole is around −60°F. The snow builds up because it is too cold for it to melt. Eventually, the pressure of all the snow makes the snow at the bottom change into ice, forming glaciers. The weight of the ice in glaciers causes them to flow downhill, often following former river valleys.

▲ Rocky moraines form a striped pattern where glaciers meet.

Ice caps and ice sheets

Ice caps form when the ice is so thick that the mountains are almost totally buried. Ice sheets are even larger, and cover most of Greenland and Antarctica. The Antarctic ice sheet is the largest in the world, and is 2.5 miles thick in places. Where it reaches the coast, towering ice shelves over 300 feet high float on the sea.

The ice in the ice caps and ice sheets moves very slowly downhill. A flake of snow at the South Pole may take thousands of years to reach the ocean, but it will get there in the end.

Glaciers — scour power

Rock may be harder than ice, but glaciers carve out tons of rocks from the sides and floor of the valleys they occupy. Loose rocks become caught up in the ice, and pieces of rock are also "plucked" from the valley floor as ice freezes around them. The embedded boulders and pebbles are dragged along by the moving glacier. The glacier acts like a giant moving sheet of sandpaper.

Many mountain glaciers are 600 to more than 1,200 feet thick, so the pressure of the ice above adds to their scouring power. Pressure also bends the ice, especially where the valley curves or changes slope, causing deep crevasses to open up. The ice insulates the bottom of the glacier from the cold air above. A thin film of meltwater (melted ice) helps the ice slip over the rocks.

Ribbons of rocks

Rocks in mountain areas are continually being broken up by frost action. The jagged fragments of rock tumble down the mountainsides and fall on to the glacier, forming dirty stripes of stones on its surface. These are called moraines.

Horace's ladder

In 1788 Horace de Saussure, the Swiss physicist, lost an iron ladder on an Alpine glacier. It was found 44 years later 1,410 feet lower down — proof that glaciers move.

Corries

Many glaciers start in hollows called corries, or cirques, where ice accumulates until it is thick enough to move downhill. Where the ice pulls away from the mountainside, a deep crack, or crevasse, called the bergschrund, forms. Meltwater trickling down this crevasse in summer, then refreezing, breaks up the rock, deepening the corrie and cutting back its rock face.

▲ If several corries develop on the same mountain, the peak may be cut into a pyramid shape, with corries separated by ridges of rock. Such peaks are called horns.

Hanging valleys and misfit streams

When glaciers finally melt, they leave huge U-shaped valleys. Streams run through them, far too small to have carved out such large valleys. Large glaciers wear away their valleys more quickly than small glaciers in side valleys. When the ice finally melts, these side valleys are left as hanging valleys, far above the main valley floor. Often waterfalls cascade hundreds of feet into the main valley below.

▲ This U-shaped valley in Switzerland was carved by a glacier when the climate was colder.

Ice ages

In the recent past over 30 percent of the Earth's surface was under ice, and many of today's landscapes were shaped by the ice. Ice ages have occurred several times in the past, when the climate cooled. The last ice age started about 2 to 3 million years ago. At its peak, ice sheets covered much of the northern hemisphere, as well as parts of Australia, New Zealand and South America. Ice reached as far as Cincinnati in the United States, and Bristol and London in the British Isles.

During an ice age, the ice advances and retreats several times. The warm periods when the ice retreats are called interglacials, and it is likely that the Earth is in an interglacial period right now. The ice sheets started retreating about 20,000 years ago. Large areas of Canada and northern Europe are covered in boulders and other debris dropped by the melting ice.

Ice age landscapes

Death of a glacier

As a glacier creeps down a valley, it eventually reaches a point where the air is warm enough for the ice to melt. When this happens, all the rocks and sand it is carrying are dropped on the land. Some of these are swept away by meltwater rivers, but the rest remains near the end of the glacier. The glacier carries bands of rock fragments called moraines. The moraines along its edges have fallen on to the ice from the valley sides. The glacier also pushes in front of it a loose assortment of soil and rubble. This forms a band across the valley where the glacier melts, often damming up the meltwater to form a lake.

Glacier meltwater is gray or greenish. This is because it contains tiny particles of rock flour — rock which has been ground to a powder under the glacier.

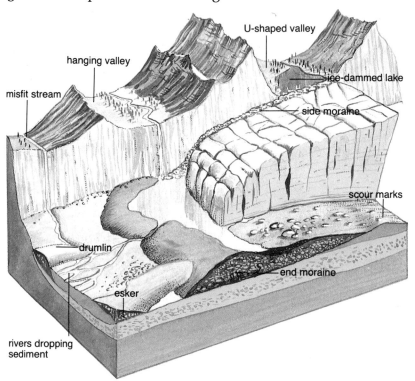

When a glacier is retreating as the climate warms, it may leave a series of end moraines. The moraines at the sides of the glacier are left as ridges along the valley. As the surface of the glacier melts, the water trickles down through crevasses and finds its way to the valley floor below. Here it runs in tunnels under the ice, dropping its sediments in long ribbons called eskers, which eventually form long, low hills.

Basket of eggs

Sometimes the glacier drops its load as clusters of streamlined mounds, 0.5 to 1 mile long, about 160 feet high, called drumlins. The hummocky country they form is nicknamed "basket of eggs" country.

Rising land

Ice sheets can be up to 2.5 miles thick, a tremendous weight of ice. When they cover large areas of the Earth's crust, the crust sags under the weight. When ice sheets melt, the land slowly rises again. Around the shores of northern Europe and North America, you can find old beaches many feet above the present sea level. These beaches were formed at sea level, but the sea is now far below them. In many places the land is still rising today.

Falling sea

A great deal of the Earth's water is locked up in ice sheets and glaciers. At the peak of the last ice age, the sea level was about 500 feet lower than today. Many shallow seas, such as the North Sea between the British Isles and Europe and the Bering Sea between Asia and Alaska, were once dry land.

After the ice

Until about 20,000 years ago, much of Canada and northern Europe, and parts of Asia, Australia and New Zealand were covered in ice sheets hundreds of feet thick. Since then, the ice sheets have melted. Today, they remain only in Greenland and Antarctica, but there are small ice caps and many glaciers in polar regions and high mountains.

When the ice retreated, the earth, rocks and sand it had picked up from the ground below, or which fell on to it from the surrounding hills, were deposited on the land in a layer hundreds of feet thick. Deposits of ice-rounded boulders and pebbles embedded in sand or clay cover much of Canada and northern Europe. Sometimes they form a gentle, rolling landscape, sometimes flat, sandy plains where the meltwater rivers flooded over the surrounding land. Farther north, the land was scoured clean of soil, and there are large stretches of bare rock, polished by the ice. Softer rocks were worn into hollows, now filled with lakes.

Frozen history

The polar ice sheets are like frozen history books. They trap and preserve the tiniest traces of dust and chemicals. Studies of the Antarctic ice show that far more dust fell on it during the peak of the last ice age than falls on it now. So it must have been very windy then. Bands of volcanic dust tell of the past activities of volcanoes. Ice also preserves radioactive fallout from nuclear tests, even lead from car exhausts.

Wandering rocks

Very large boulders can be carried by ice sheets, either embedded in the ice or dragged along the bed of the ice sheet. Today, these "erratics" rest in fields and on hilltops, landmarks of rock from faraway lands.

◄ Meltwater from glaciers and ice sheets spreads out over the surrounding land in a network of gleaming rivers.

Did you know?

The polar ice caps hold 2 percent of the Earth's water, enough to raise the level of the oceans by 200 feet if they melted.

The Antarctic ice is the best place to look for meteorites, since they are the only rocks there.

There are many lakes under the Antarctic ice. Why do you think this is? Answer on page 150.

More about glaciers (pp.46, 47);
meteorites (pp.139, 144)

49

Soil

The origin of soil

Soil is produced by the breakdown of rocks. These may be solid rocks, or they may be loose masses of rock fragments, stones and sand left on the land by rivers, ice sheets, glaciers or the sea. The rocks are broken down by frost, heat and water.

As soon as plants can take root, their roots help to bind the soil particles together. The plants protect the soil against wind and rain, and help it build up faster. When they die, plants decay and their rotting remains sink into the soil. Bacteria and fungi in the soil help to break them down, producing a dark brown substance, called humus. Humus is an amorphous substance that absorbs water, and tends to stick to soil particles, binding them together. As the humus decays, vital mineral salts are released into the soil, where plants can take them up. Organic acids, produced by soil organisms, seep down in the rainwater to the rocks below and help to break them down further.

▲ Laterite soil is common in the tropics.

Soils around the world

The climate, especially the amount of rainfall and evaporation, has a big effect on the soil. Where rainfall is heavy, mineral salts and humus are washed out of the soil, which becomes pale and sterile.

In warm climates, evaporation draws water and dissolved mineral salts back up to the surface between rainstorms. In the tropics, these salts form a hard layer of iron and aluminum oxides which prevents rain soaking into the soil. This gives these "laterite" soils a reddish color.

Soil shapes the landscape

Soil affects the appearance of the countryside. In deserts, where there is very little soil, the outlines of the hills are sharp and angular. In grassland, with deep fertile soil, the hills and valleys are soft and rounded shapes. Deserts are yellow and brown, the colors of bare rock, while grasslands and woodlands are green with plants.

Soils from the wind

Dust particles are very small and light, and can be blown for thousands of miles. If the dust is eventually deposited in thick layers, it forms a very fertile yellow soil, called loess. The loess in northern China is 1,000 feet thick in places, and has been blown there from the Gobi Desert.

Plants protect the soil

If the surface of the soil is left to dry out, it, too, is likely to be blown away. Usually a layer of plants binds the soil together, and helps to retain moisture so that it does not dry out. Where forests are cleared in areas which have little rainfall, the soil soon dries out and is washed down hill slopes, or blown away, creating deserts.

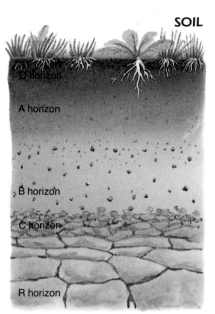

The soil profile

If you dig a deep pit and look at the soil from the surface to the solid rock below, you are looking at a soil profile. Most soils have very distinct layers, called horizons:

O **(organic) horizon** dark brown decaying remains of plants and soil animals such as earthworms, beetles and ants.

A **horizon** (topsoil) rich in humus. Rainwater dissolves minerals and carries them deeper, leaving the soil here a grayish color. This process is called leaching.

B **horizon** less humus, but minerals from the A horizon are deposited here. If there is plenty of air in the soil, iron oxides form, giving a yellow or reddish-brown color. Sometimes so much iron is deposited that it forms a hard layer called a pan, which does not allow water through.

C **horizon** partly decomposed rock fragments. Here, rock is still breaking down.

R **(rock) horizon** the parent rock.

The rock breakers

Lichens, curious combinations of algae and fungi, are often the first organisms to live on bare rock. Lichens grow very slowly, so they do not need many nutrients. They produce chemicals which help to break down and loosen the rock surface, creating the beginnings of soil.

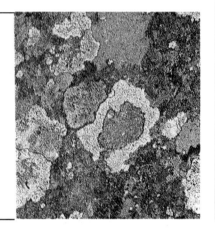

Animals are important, too

Ten square feet of fertile soil contains more than 1 billion animals, from microscopic one-celled creatures to insects, worms and large burrowing animals like rabbits, moles and mice. When they die, the nutrients locked up in their bodies escape into the soil as they decay, and enrich it.

Welcome worms

Earthworms are important soil animals. They allow air into the soil through their tunnels, and help water drain through it. They drag down leaves into the soil, where they rot and add to the humus. Their droppings contain nitrogen, which plants need, and minerals.

Did you know?

In the American Midwest during the 1930s, millions of tons of soil were blown away from ploughed land before new crops could be grown on it. The area came to be known as the Dust Bowl.

Earthworms can move 10 tons of soil per hectare per year.

More about earthworms (p.39); nutrients and decay (pp.132, 133)

The work of the wind

The power of the wind

The wind may be quiet and invisible, yet it is astonishingly powerful. It can blow down trees, lift off roofs, and carry sand and dust for vast distances. Scientists have calculated that a strong windstorm can carry up to a million tons of material for more than 1,800 miles.

▲ Landscape Arch, in the Arches National Park, Utah, is the longest natural arch in the world. It is made of natural sandstone and spans 280 feet across the canyon.

Jumping sand

Once the wind has a load of sand, it can actually attack the rocks. The sand blown against the rocks helps to break them down, just as builders blow high-power jets of air laden with sand at buildings to clean the walls of dirt or loose plaster.

Fine clay particles can be carried high in the atmosphere, but sand grains are heavier, and the wind cannot lift them much above 5 feet. They bounce along the ground, bumping into each other, rebounding off rock surfaces and rolling down slopes. Even small stones can be bounced along the ground by strong winds. The rocks are worn away up to a height of about 5 feet by this sandblasting. Harder rocks are worn away more slowly than soft ones, and the bare hills of many deserts are sculptured into fascinating shapes by the wind. Strange, mushroom-shaped "pedestals" are formed when hard rock lies on softer rock, which is worn away faster. Caves form in soft-rock cliffs.

Blowing away the rocks

A wind carrying no hard materials will make little impression on solid rock. But once the outer layers of the rocks have been broken down by heat, frost or chemical processes, the loose material can be picked up and carried away by the wind as sand and dust. If the surface of the soil dries out, it is likely to be blown away as well.

What is sand?

Rocks are made up of mineral crystals. When they are broken down, some of the minerals dissolve in rainwater and are carried away. Soft materials soon disintegrate into fine dust. Harder ones form larger particles, called sand. Sand is mostly made up of a very hard mineral called quartz.

▲ A large mushroom-shaped rock pedestal.

Piling up the sand

Where there is lots of sand on the move, the wind piles it up into great heaps or hills, called dunes. Sand is carried by wind in much the same way as by water. The faster the wind moves, the larger the grains it can carry. If the wind speed drops, the larger grains are dropped.

As a dune builds up, it eventually becomes unstable, and sand on the sheltered side avalanches, forming a steep slope. The other side has a gentler slope.

▲ When the wind meets an obstacle, like a dune or a large rock, the air stream is disturbed. Some air flows to either side of the obstacle, leaving a "wind shadow" in front and behind it. In the wind shadow, wind speed is less and sand is dropped.

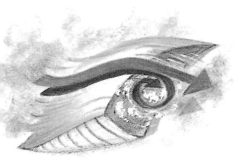

▲ After the wind passes over the crest of a dune, the wind pressure falls, and a small eddy curls back up the sheltered side, helping to keep it steep. Ripples on the surface of dunes are formed in much the same way, but on a smaller scale.

▲ Dunes and ripples are shaped by the wind.

Dunes without sand

The wind piles up snow to form snowdrifts in much the same way as it makes sand dunes. In some places there are dunes made entirely of salt crystals or shell fragments.

Smooth sand

The sand itself is worn down by millions of collisions with other sand grains. Wind-blown sand has rounded edges and a frosted appearance, unlike river-borne sand grains, which tend to be more angular. Pebbles in the desert are sometimes pyramid-shaped, with several flattened faces. These "ventifacts" (meaning made by the wind) are formed where the wind direction varies, and the pebbles are worn away on first one side, then another.

Did you know?

Wind-blown dust on the island of Barbados in the Caribbean contains minerals from Europe and Africa, thousands of miles away across the Atlantic Ocean.

The highest recorded wind speed is 231 mph at Mount Washington, in New Hampshire.

The windiest place on Earth is the George V Coast, Antarctica.

More about wind (pp.34, 55); crystals (pp.14, 15)

Deserts

What makes a desert?

About 30 percent of the surface of the continents is desert. Some deserts are cut off from rain-bearing winds by mountain ranges. Others occur in the tropics and subtropics, where the air is always dry. The high temperatures cause what little water there is to evaporate before it can sink far into the ground. Cold deserts are found in the polar regions and on high mountains, where the ground is frozen and there is little free water.

Most deserts receive less than 1 inch of rain a year on average. But this is not the true picture. Many deserts have no rain for several years, then get a torrential downpour. Rain in deserts can be very patchy. Isolated thunderstorms can drench one area, while another only 60 miles away remains dry.

▲ The Devil's Marbles, Northern Territory, in Australia are examples of "onion-skin" rocks.

▶ Desert pebbles and gravels are often coated in a dark, shiny, brown "varnish." This contains iron and manganese. Nobody is quite sure how it forms.

Desert muds often have a coat of salt, left behind when the water evaporated at the surface. This picture shows salt-coated cracks in the Namib Desert, Namibia (South West Africa).

Blowing hot and cold

Deserts suffer extremes of temperature. By day, they get very hot because there is no cloud cover to filter out the Sun, and no vegetation to give shade. But at night, the lack of clouds means that heat radiates back into the atmosphere rapidly, and it can be not much above freezing point, even in the tropics.

Onion-skin rocks

Rocks do not transmit heat very well. In hot sun, the outer layer of the rock quickly gets hot and expands, but the inner layers remain cool and un-expanded. These pressures cause layers of rock to peel off, rather like the skin of an onion, forming a rounded, flaky surface.

Rusting rocks

Many rocky deserts are reddish or rusty brown. This is because the oxygen in the air reacts with rocks. Rocks containing iron turn a rusty brown when exposed to the air, as the iron reacts with the oxygen to form iron oxides. Compare the color of the Devil's Marbles with the color of the laterite soil on page 50.

Carved out by water

Surprisingly, much of the erosion of rocks in deserts is done by water. When rain does fall, it is very heavy, and causes fast-flowing floods. Because there are few plants, there is not much soil, and the rain is not absorbed by the ground but runs off down the slopes. It funnels into the valleys, forming "flash floods," which can be six feet deep. They can carry large boulders that scour the valleys into deep steep-sided gorges called wadis.

Where the wadis leave the hills, the floods spread out on the plains, and the sand and pebbles they carry are dropped in conelike alluvial fans at the foot of the hills. The water trickles on across the plains, now much shallower, and evaporates rapidly. Often it ends up in shallow lakes with no outlets, called salinas. Here the water evaporates, and layers of salt remain.

Oases

Sudden patches of vegetation, and even trees, are found where there is water not far below the surface. This can happen if water, which has soaked into nearby mountains, drains down through the rocks under the desert and becomes trapped by a hard waterproof layer of rock. The beds of wadis, although dry for most of the time, may also cut down deep enough to come close to this water. They are often dotted with trees.

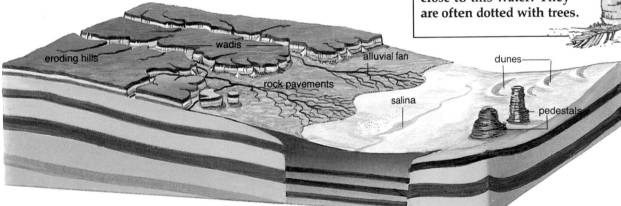

eroding hills · wadis · rock pavements · alluvial fan · salina · dunes · pedestals

Sculptured by the wind

The wind also helps to sculpture the desert. Most people think deserts are full of sand dunes. But in fact, only about 20 percent of the deserts have dunes. They are formed where wind laden with sand slows down and drops its load. Some desert dunes reach heights of 650 feet or more. In most deserts, the wind blows the sand and soil away, leaving gravel plains or bare rock surfaces, called rock pavements.

Sand is formed when rocks break down. The wind picks it up and blows it away, leaving behind the bare rocks. The sand scours the rocks it blows against, wearing them away. Soft rocks are worn away faster than hard ones, and where soft and hard rocks occur together, fantastic shapes are carved, such as the mushroom-shaped pedestal you can see in the picture on page 52.

—Did you know?—

The world's largest desert is the Sahara Desert, 3.2 million square miles.

Each year the deserts of the world spread by 20,000 square miles.

In winter the temperature of the Libyan Desert fluctuates from 100°F by day to 33°F at night.

More about deserts (p.123)

Mountaintop and tundra

The tundra

In the far north, between the regions of everlasting ice and snow and the dark northern forests, there is a vast area of gently rolling land, carpeted with mosses, lichens and low-growing shrubs. This is the tundra. No trees grow here, and in winter the land is blanketed in snow. Winter temperatures reach −25°F, but in the long summer days, the tundra may warm to 122°F.

Similar treeless wasteland occurs on some of the highest mountaintops in more temperate climates. The climate here is kinder, with cooler summers and warmer winters.

Pingos

In parts of the tundra there are strange mounds of earth, up to 300 feet high and 2,600 feet across. Each contains a core of blue-white ice. Some have a spring flowing from the top; others have a crater filled with a small lake. Pingos are formed when water below the ground is forced upward by the pressure of ice advancing through the soil around it.

A deep, deep frost
Less than 1 inch below the surface, the tundra is frozen all year round. This permanently frozen ground is called permafrost. In parts of Siberia, the permafrost reaches down to 2,300 feet. Water cannot pass through ice, so any water formed by melting snow collects on the surface in pools and lakes. This explains why the tundra is dotted with lakes, although it receives less rain (or snow) than many deserts — only about 8 inches a year.

The rolling stones
Tundra and mountaintop suffer from frost for much of the year. Frost is responsible for the appearance of a lot of stones on the ground. Water expands as it freezes. If water gets into cracks in the rocks, it can shatter them into pieces as it freezes.

When chilled by the cold night air, the bottom of a stone cools more rapidly than the mud around it, and ice starts to form. As the water freezes and expands, it lifts the stone up. Where the ground slopes, the stone may topple and roll downhill when the ice melts.

Dangerous summits

The summit, or top, of a mountain can be a dangerous place. Frost breaks up the surface of the rocks, which crumble away underfoot. Rock fragments tumble downhill to form loose piles of stones called screes. Mountains are exposed to very strong winds, 95 mph and more. These can bring storms with them. The rapidly changing cloud cover means that the temperature can change very quickly indeed. You can be standing in sunshine in summer clothing one minute, and five minutes later find yourself in a swirling snowstorm. Cloud and mist can close in on a mountaintop very quickly. In a few minutes, the distance you can see may fall from 60 miles to 10 feet. The air gets thinner as you go higher up a mountain, so there is less oxygen, and breathing becomes difficult.

▲ Patterns of stones on the tundra are caused by frost action.

Stripes and polygons

Parts of the tundra are covered with stones set in strange patterns, called polygons. The temperature drops so sharply in winter that the ground shrinks and cracks. Water seeps into these cracks and freezes, widening the cracks as it expands. This makes the ground between the cracks break up into many-sided blocks. When the soil expands again in summer, it swells up to form hummocks, and the loose stones of the surface roll down into the cracks. Some stone polygons are over 300 feet across, separated by cracks up to 10 feet deep. Where the ground slopes, the polygon pattern changes into stripes as the stones roll downhill. Stripes and polygons are also found on gently sloping mountaintops.

Avalanches

Mountains get many snowstorms in a winter. Often the surface of the snow melts by day, then freezes at night to form a layer of ice. The next snowstorm will produce another layer of snow, until the slopes are coated in many layers of snow and ice. Snow layers easily slip on the ice below, especially when it starts to melt, and can break away and thunder down the mountainside as avalanches.

The creeping Earth

When the surface layers of the tundra soil melt in summer, they tend to slide over the frozen permafrost below. Any slight slope is enough to set the soil creeping slowly downward. On mountaintops, the steeply sloping surface increases the soil creep. Any obstacle in its path, such as a stone or a tuft of grass, is enough to make the soil collect above it. These piles of soil form narrow terraces that are often mistaken for sheep tracks.

More about clouds (pp.80, 81); cold climates (pp.86, 87)

Lakes

Natural dams

Many lakes are formed where rivers are dammed by ice or rock. Glaciers, landslides and lava flows can all be natural dams. At the coast, bars of sand or pebbles create lagoons between the shore and the sea.

Rocky lake basins form when ice scours away the softer rocks. Where ice sheets and rivers shed their loads of sediment over the surrounding land, lakes fill hollows in the sediments. Much bigger lake basins are formed by large scale upheavals of the Earth's crust.

▲ This lake has formed in a hollow carved by a glacier. It is held in by a dam of sediment deposited by the melting glacier. An outlet stream is slowly cutting its way through the dam.

Death of a lake

No lake lasts forever. Rivers bring in sand and silt. When a river enters the still waters of a lake, it drops its load of sediment, often forming a fan-shaped pile of sediment which grows out into the lake. Finer particles of silt are carried farther, eventually sinking to the bottom to form layers of mud. Over thousands of years, sediments hundreds of feet thick can accumulate in large lakes, gradually filling them up.

Plants growing around the lake shore trap mud between their roots, slowly building the shore out into the lake. Most lakes have a river flowing out of them. As it flows, the river slowly cuts down through the rock which is damming the lake. As the dam is lowered, the water escapes and the lake becomes shallower.

Deep water

Rainwater can often seep into rocks between the rock particles. It moves down through the rock until it reaches a level where the rock is already full of water. This level is called the water table. Wherever the water table is at the surface, a lake will form if the water cannot run away down a slope or into a river.

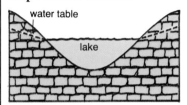

Some rocks have no spaces for the water to seep into — they are impermeable rocks. Here, the water table is at the surface, and the land is dotted with lakes and pools. Frozen layers of soil also act like impermeable rocks. Other rocks have plenty of spaces for water, but lie on top of impermeable rocks, so they soon fill up with water. This also brings the water table close to the surface.

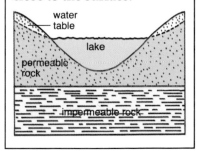

The thermocline

When the surface waters of a lake are warmed by the Sun, they become less dense than the cooler water below, so they tend to float on it. This warm layer may extend to depths of 600 to 3,000 feet. It does not mix with the cooler water below. We call this layering the thermocline. Above this level, winds mix the surface waters.

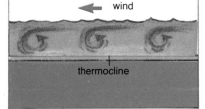

In the tropics, the thermocline is more or less permanent. Temperate and polar regions have no thermocline in winter, when storms mix the water to a great depth.

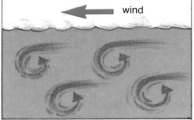

This allows nutrients, released from decaying organisms that have sunk to the bottom, to be brought back up to the surface, where they can be used for food by plants and animals. Thermoclines also occur in the oceans.

Beneath the surface

In deep lakes, many changes occur as you travel from the surface to the bottom. The light fades rapidly, and the temperature falls. Deep down, the temperature does not change much, while at the surface the water is quickly heated by the Sun, or cooled by contact with cold air. In winter, a layer of ice may form, protecting the water below from cooling, and allowing plant and animal life to survive under the ice.

▲ This lake is slowly being filled in by sediment deposited by the inflowing river.

Salt lakes

If a lake is in a hot climate, water evaporates from its surface. The dissolved mineral salts brought in by rivers become more and more concentrated, until some become solid crystals. In some deserts, the lake may dry out completely between rainstorms. Then only the layers of salt crystals remain.

Did you know?

The largest freshwater lake is Lake Superior, with a surface area of 31,000 square miles.

The largest saltwater lake is the Caspian Sea, with an area of 141,000 square miles.

Beavers create lakes by damming rivers with branches and mud. Their dams can be over 300 feet long and 10 feet high.

More about ox bow lakes (p.44); saltwater lakes (pp. 22, 127)

59

The angry sea

The battle of the beaches

When you draw a map of the world, you are really drawing the pattern of its coastlines. Ten thousand years ago this map would have looked quite different. This is because the position and shape of the coasts are always changing. In some places the sea is winning, and the land is retreating. In other places, sand and mud banks grow out into the sea, and eventually become new land.

Hammers of water

It may seem surprising that water can carve cliffs and caves from solid rock. The force of a large breaking wave is enormous, like dropping a 10-ton weight on 10 square feet of rock. Storm waves are even stronger, and can move blocks of rock weighing more than 1,000 tons.

Waves also blast the rocks. When a wave pounds against cracks in the rocks, the air inside is squeezed very hard. When the wave retreats, this air expands rapidly, acting rather like a small charge of dynamite inside the crack.

▲ The sea has cut a rocky platform at the base of the cliffs.

Retreating cliffs

The pounding waves wear away the base of the cliffs, until the upper part of the cliff hangs out over space. The weight of this overhanging rock puts a great strain on the cliffs, and large sections break away and fall into the sea. Here they are broken up by the waves and provide further ammunition for attacking the remaining cliffs.

When a wave breaks on the shore, it rushes forward as frothy surf, then drains back down the beach as the "backwash," dragging pebbles with it. Where the rocks are very hard, this can wear away a bare rocky platform.

Storms change the map

During a bad storm, the sea can cause more damage than it does all year, especially if the storm coincides with high tide. Storm waves, of great height and speed, may have traveled thousands of miles across the oceans. During a storm, the sea level can be raised over 5 feet. Beaches are stripped of sand and pebbles, and protective lines of sand dunes may be swept away.

In 1953, a severe storm caused disastrous flooding of eastern England and the Netherlands. At Covehithe in England, the coast was cut back 90 feet, and 3.3 million tons of rock fell down in just 24 hours.

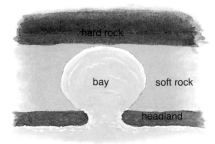

The shaping of the coasts

Soft rocks wear away faster than hard rocks. Hard bands of rock stand out as headlands, while softer rocks form sheltered bays. The waves pound hardest on the headlands. Over a long period of time, the headlands are worn back, and the coastline becomes smoother.

The sea attacks a headland from both sides. Rocks with large natural cracks in them, like limestones, often have caves carved in them by the sea. The roof of a cave may collapse, forming a blowhole through which spray shoots as the waves rush into the cave below. Where caves on both sides of a headland eventually join, a natural arch is formed. Often the top of the arch collapses, forming stacks — pillars of rock separated from the cliffs.

▲ A natural arch on the coast of Pembrokeshire, Wales.

Rias and fjords

During the peak of the ice age, about 20,000 years ago, the sea level was much lower than it is today. Since then, the sea level has risen, flooding former river valleys. These drowned river valleys, called rias, are found on the west coasts of North America and Europe.

Where the valleys have been greatly deepened by glaciers, they form long inlets called fjords, whose walls drop almost vertically into the water. The floor of the old valley may be hundreds of feet below the water surface.

Pounding pebbles

Rock boulders and pebbles broken from the cliffs are hurled at the rocks by the waves, then dragged back across the shore as the waves retreat. As well as pounding the base of the cliffs, the pebbles themselves are worn down by colliding with each other. Their corners are worn away, and they become smooth and rounded.

Did you know?

The world has 194,000 miles of coastlines.

Some coastal sand dunes are over 150 feet high.

On Martha's Vineyard, an island off the coast of Massachusetts, the cliffs are retreating by 5.6 feet a year. A lighthouse has had to be moved three times.

More about beachcombing (pp.66, 67); the ice ages (pp.47, 48, 49)

61

The gentle coasts

Building beaches

All around the world, rivers carry trillions of tons of sand and silt into the sea every year. These are picked up by the waves, and carried along the coast by currents until the water reaches a sheltered area. There it drops its load to form beaches. On rocky coasts, waves pounding at the cliffs shatter the rocks into boulders and pebbles, which are also rolled along by the sea. Some tropical beaches are made almost entirely of broken shells and coral washed up from nearby reefs.

Sand dunes

Where the wind usually blows toward the shore, it may drive the sand up the beach and pile into it into dunes. As sand piles up on the seaward side of a dune, it topples over the top and down the other side, so the dunes slowly move inland. New dunes form on the beach, and the dunes may multiply to form a sandy coastal plain.

Certain types of plant are very good at taking root in sand dunes. They can grow fast enough to avoid being buried, and their roots help to bind the sand together. The plants themselves help to trap more sand, and their dead remains sink into the surface of the dune, and start to form a soil. This encourages new kinds of plants to grow, especially if there is plenty of rainfall. Eventually the dunes may become covered in vegetation and stop moving.

Sorting out the pebbles

When a wave breaks on the beach, the water rushes up the beach, taking shingle and sand with it. The water drains back down the beach in the backwash. But the backwash is weak, and cannot carry the larger pebbles, so they remain farther up the beach. Sand, then silt, is dropped farther down the beach. At low tide, you can sometimes see where the sandy beach changes to mud flats.

Danger behind the waves

Water is moved along the coast by currents as well as waves. Where waves and currents push water up the beach, another current, the undertow, flows away from the beach, taking the water back. On some beaches, this invisible current is very strong, and very dangerous to swimmers.

▲ Marram grass on the dunes.

Drifting sands

Waves are caused by the wind blowing over the surface of the sea. The angle at which the waves hit the beach depends upon the wind direction and the shape of the coast. When waves approach the beach at an angle, the pebbles and sand are washed up the beach with the water. But the backwash flows straight back to sea, so the sand and pebbles follow a zigzag course along the beach in the direction of the prevailing (usual) wind. This is called the longshore drift.

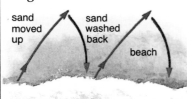

sand moved up

sand washed back

beach

waves approach shore at an angle

Where the longshore drift meets an obstacle, such as a headland or a large rock, the sand or shingle piles up against it, starting to build up a beach. You can see this movement of sand where people have built long fences, called groynes, down the beach to slow down the sand movement. Sand piles up on one side of the groyne.

Spits and lagoons

If the coastline is not straight, the longshore drift may continue in a straight line, even where the coast curves. Then it can form long ridges of sand or shingle called spits. Often the end of a spit is curved toward the shore by currents.

Some spits stretch from one headland to the next, enclosing a shallow lake called a lagoon. Where the sea breaks through a spit, barrier islands can be formed. Some coasts have miles of spits and barrier islands, separated from the land by long lagoons. They help to protect the coast from the sea. Some of the longest beaches in the world are formed in the shelter of spits.

▲ Groynes trap drifting sand.

— Did you know? —

Some beaches look quite different in winter and summer. In winter, storm waves remove material from the beach faster than waves can bring more. The beach becomes narrower, more pebbly and less sandy. In spring, it slowly widens and becomes sandy again. In parts of California, the beach widens by 200 feet in summer.

More about currents (pp.76, 77); waves (pp.60, 75)

Where rivers meet the sea

Rivers change the map

The shape of the coast can change dramatically where a river enters the sea. A river carries a load of sand and silt gathered up as it carves out its valley from the surrounding rocks. When it reaches the sea, it slows down, and drops much of its load. The sand and silt may form large fans of sediment, called deltas, which push the coast seaward; or it may build ridges across the river mouth. Sometimes the sea invades the river mouth, forming a deep funnel-shaped bay called an estuary.

Patterns in the sand

There are many fascinating patterns in the sand and mud of an estuary. The commonest are rows of ripples, formed by the action of the tide. Water can move sand grains, just like the wind does, to form miniature dunes and ripples. In some estuaries, the pattern of currents produces sand dunes on the riverbed that change positions with every tide.

Often the currents that form when the tide is coming in are different from those present when the tide is going out (ebbing). They cut different channels in the sand and mud, forming complicated patterns.

If the mud dries out at low tide, it cracks. The pattern of mud cracks varies. The mud may shrink into many-sided blocks, or it may form curly flakes instead.

Salt and sand

Estuaries are hard places for plants and animals to live in. When the tide is in, they are full of salt water. When the tide is out, they contain just fresh river water. At low tide, large areas of mud and sand are no longer covered by water. The mud dries out in the sunshine, and the mudflat can become very hot, since there are no tall plants to shade it. As the water evaporates, its salt concentration rises, so animals that live there, such as snails and worms, have to be able to live in very high salt concentrations as well as in fresh water. Most of them live buried in the mud, emerging to feed when the tide is coming in. The amount of salt can change very quickly if heavy rain falls after the mudflat has dried out.

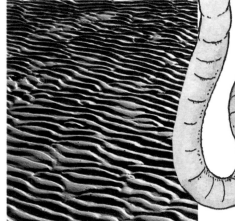

▲ Ripples at low tide.

Mudflats and salt marshes

Estuaries are strongly affected by the tides. At high tide, sea water flows a long way up the estuary. At low tide, the water level is much lower, and the water itself is mainly fresh river water. Tides are not the same the world over. In some places they rise and fall by less than 3 feet; in others the difference can be 50 feet.

Where there is a strong inrushing of water on the rising tide, sand and mud are swept into the estuary by the sea. The falling tide has less power, and cannot remove all the sediment it brought in. Mud banks build up along the sides of the estuary, sometimes for a mile or so inland. Large areas of mud collect where there is a bend in the estuary, because the water flows more slowly on the inside of the bend and drops more sediment.

In time, plants take hold on the mud, trapping more mud among their roots and stems. This builds up the banks until they form flat stretches of dry land. Now a closer cover of plants can grow on them. These flats are still covered by salt water during the highest tides of the year — they are salt marshes. Only a few kinds of plants can grow in these conditions, but salt marshes make good pasture for cattle and horses.

▲ Mangrove swamps in Brunei.

Tides and bores

Very long estuaries act like funnels, squeezing the incoming tide into a narrower and narrower channel. In places which get very high tides, the incoming tide forms a bore — a wall of water that rolls up the estuary like a wave. The largest bore in the world is on the Ch'ient'ang'kian River in eastern China. It reaches 25 feet in height, and travels at 15 to 17 mph.

Mangrove swamps

In the warmer parts of the world, muddy estuaries and coasts are often covered in mangrove swamps. Mangroves are trees which can live in salty water. They put out a vast spreading network of roots through the mud. This helps to support the trees and also traps more mud. Plant roots need air to breathe. Mangroves produce roots above the ground to take in air. Some put down long curving roots which reach from high up on their trunks to the mud below. Others stick up "elbows" of roots above the mud. Mangrove swamps slowly advance seaward as they trap more and more mud and sand, and build up the land.

More about deltas (p. 45); tides (pp. 74, 75)

65

Beachcombing

Nature's history book

Beaches are like pages of a history book. Bare cliffs, pebbles and sand can all tell us about the Earth's history. Cliffs are good places to look for fossils, especially at the bottom, where the sea is continually exposing new rock surfaces.

Limestone is often slowly dissolved away around a fossil, so the fossils in limestone rocks may actually stick out from the surface. In other sedimentary rocks, the best place to look is along the bedding planes. Bedding planes were formed where the sediments that made the rocks were worn away by wind or water, before new sediments were laid down on top. They show up as dark lines or thin cracks in the rocks.

Look carefully at objects you find on the beach. Some fossils look much like creatures you can find alive today. Turtle shells, snail shells, starfish, and sharks' teeth are easily overlooked. In some places you can find fossil wood. Do not forget to look for trace fossils — the tracks of worms and footprints of animals in fossilized mud and sand.

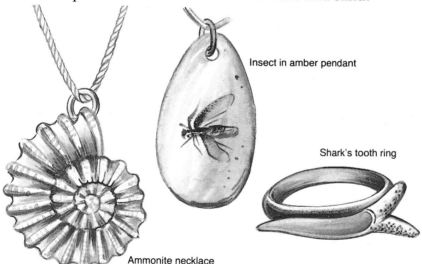

Insect in amber pendant

Shark's tooth ring

Ammonite necklace

▲ Attractive gifts can be made from fossils.

Fossil presents

Large fossils with an attractive coat of varnish make good paperweights. Some fossils can be made into necklaces by boring a hole in the middle and threading them on a piece of string or a leather cord. It is quite easy to make jewelry from your polished stones too. You can buy metal settings in which to stick them. There are very strong glues called epoxy resins for sticking rocks to metal.

Insects in amber

On some beaches, you can find pieces of yellow or orange amber, with insects beautifully preserved in them. The insects were trapped in the sticky resin when it first oozed out of tree trunks long ago.

Sand pictures

To make a sand picture, you need a piece of hardboard. Draw your picture on the board. Now smear a fine layer of glue over the areas you need to cover with a particular colored sand. Sprinkle the sand over the glue using a tea strainer. Wait for the glue to dry completely, then shake off the loose sand before starting on the next color. Later on, you can varnish part of your picture for added effect.

Pebble pictures

To make pebble pictures, draw a picture on a piece of hardboard, then stick your pebbles to it with a strong glue. To avoid getting glue on your precious pebbles, use a pair of tweezers to handle them.

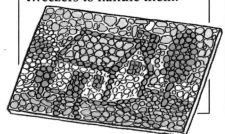

Hidden beauty

When rocks are exposed to the air, chemical reactions take place between the minerals in the rocks and the oxygen in the air. This makes the rocks change color, and they look rather dull. If you chip a piece off a rock, you will find it is a different color underneath. You can get some pleasant surprises by breaking pebbles in half with a hammer. If you use a hand lens or powerful magnifying glass, you will be able to see crystals in the rocks. The best minerals and crystals are found in igneous and metamorphic rocks.

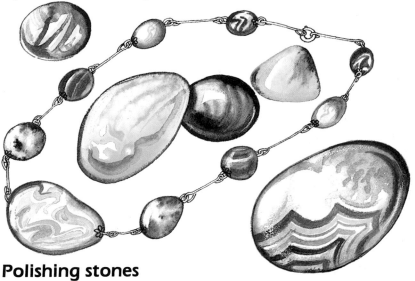

Polishing stones

Pebbles often look much more attractive when wet than when dry. You can recapture this effect by varnishing them. You can buy easy-to-use spray cans of varnish. The attractive polished rocks and minerals used in jewelry are ground smooth in a machine called a tumble polisher. Books in your local library will tell you how to do this.

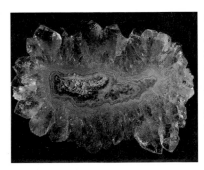

Geodes

A geode is a hollow in the rock in which very large crystals have had space to grow. Geodes often form large rounded pebbles, and reveal their treasures only when cracked in half.

Take care not to inhale the poisonous fumes from your spray can of varnish. Hold it well away from your face.

Coral reefs

Darwin's puzzle

About 150 years ago, a naturalist called Charles Darwin sailed around the world in a ship called HMS *Beagle*. His journey took nearly five years. During the trip, Darwin became fascinated by coral reefs. He was puzzled by their formation and the way the different kinds of reefs developed. His theories about coral reefs are still accepted by many scientists today.

Coral facts

Coral reefs are made of the limestone skeletons of millions of tiny animals. These are called coral polyps and have very special needs. They live only in clear, clean water. The water must have a temperature between 63°F and 95°F. They cannot grow at depths greater than 165 feet. Coral reefs are found only in tropical and subtropical seas.

There are three different kinds of coral reefs.

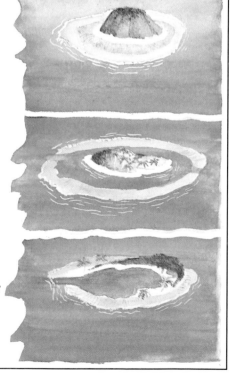

Fringing reefs grow in shallow water very close to land. They are separated from land by a narrow stretch of water that can be waded across when the tide is out.

Barrier reefs also grow parallel to the land but they are separated from land by a wide channel. The channel is deep enough for ships to pass.

Atolls are ring-shaped coral islands. In the center of the ring is an area of water called a lagoon. Atolls are often very far from land.

The story of an atoll

Charles Darwin noticed that all coral reefs were in regions where the land was known to have sunk in the past. His ideas on reef formation can be seen below.

An island surrounded by a fringing reef.

The island sinks slowly. The reef continues to grow at the same rate as the island sinks.

Over millions of years the island sinks completely. An atoll is now formed.

The Australian Great Barrier Reef is the biggest structure made by living organisms. It is over 1,200 miles long and can be seen from the Moon.

▲ A Pacific coral reef seen from the air.

Volcanoes and reef formation

Geologists have suggested other ways in which the different kinds of reefs might have been formed. There is plenty of volcanic activity on the ocean floor. Sometimes the undersea mountains produced by this activity push their peaks above the surface of the sea to form islands or chains of islands. Many of the Caribbean islands were formed in this way. On other occasions, the peaks of the new volcanoes do not quite reach the surface. In both cases, the underwater slopes near the surface are good places for corals to start growing.

▲ Coral reefs are home for many different kinds of animals and plants, all dependent on each other for food and shelter.

The reef destroyers

Coral reefs are easily damaged. Strong winds such as hurricanes and heavy waves batter the reefs and break the coral up. Even the fish and other organisms of the reefs cause damage. The coral nibblers constantly bite off small pieces of coral when they feed. Some of the nibblers turn the limestone of the coral into fine coral sand.

The crown of thorns

A species of starfish called the crown of thorns has become a very serious threat to living coral. It moves slowly over the reef, feeding on the coral polyps as it goes. It has destroyed enormous amounts of coral in the last thirty years. Huge stretches of the Great Barrier Reef have disappeared.

—Did you know?—

Lateiki Island, in the Pacific Ocean, is the world's newest volcanic island. It appeared in June 1979.

Captain Cook was once shipwrecked on the Great Barrier Reef. He did not realize he was sailing in the channel between the reef and the mainland.

More about volcanoes (pp.16, 17); volcanic islands (p.11)

The ocean floor

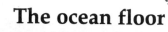

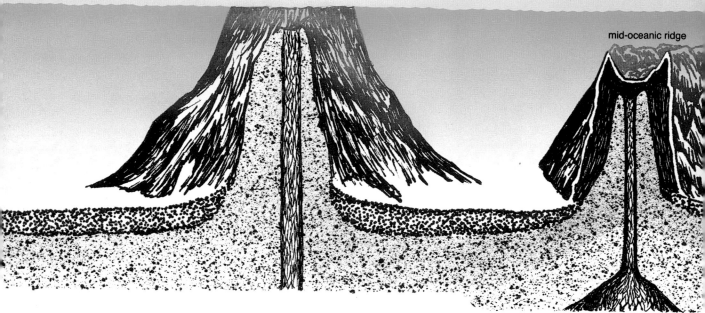

volcano

mid-oceanic ridge

At the bottom of the ocean

The bottom of the ocean is not just a wide plain of sand and sediment. In places, mountains rise from depths greater than 20,000 feet and break the surface to form islands. There are canyons and volcanoes, even sandbanks. Parts of the ocean floor are light and full of waving seaweeds. Other parts are in total darkness, with strange animals creeping through the deep mud.

The continental shelf

From the edge of the continents, the continental shelf slopes gently down to about 650 feet, covered in sand, mud and silt brought by rivers and streams. In places there are underwater sand dunes — the sand is moved by currents instead of being blown by winds.

The continental slope

At the edge of the continental shelf, the sea bed slopes steeply down to depths of 6,500 to 13,000 feet. In places the slope is broken by great canyons, some of them even bigger than the Grand Canyon. Continental slopes are the highest and longest walls on Earth.

The abyssal plains

Deeper still, 1,300 feet or more, the sea bed flattens out to wide empty plains, where there is very little life. These plains make up 75 percent of the ocean floor. They are covered in fine sediments. In the shallower parts, the skeletons of dead microscopic organisms from the water above accumulate to great depths. Some are made of lime, others of silica. In still deeper parts, red muds coat the sea bed instead, full of strange things such as sharks' teeth, whales' earbones and volcanic dust.

coral atoll

sedimentary rocks

abyssal plain

sediments

basalts

▲ A section through a typical ocean. Not drawn to scale.

Mountains under the sea

Vast mountain ranges rise from these plains, and run the length of the ocean basins. The peaks of these mid-oceanic ridges tower thousands of feet above the ocean floor. In some places, they rise above the surface of the sea to form islands like the Azores, Ascension Island and Iceland. In other places, there are isolated volcanoes, some also rising above the surface to form islands. Many extinct ocean volcanoes in the tropics are topped by coral reefs called atolls.

Birthplace of the Earth's crust

The mid-oceanic ridges are made of basalt lava. Along these ridges, lava wells up from deep in the Earth. Sometimes it quietly forms broad sheets of basalt, and sometimes it erupts violently to form volcanoes. This lava then forms new ocean floor.

Deep-sea trenches

Near the margins of the continents there are some-times deep trenches. The Mariana trench is the deepest, at over 36,000 feet. These trenches occur where the ocean floor is being forced under the continents.

Did you know?

The tallest underwater mountain rises 50,000 feet from the ocean floor. The highest mountain on land, Mount Everest, is 29,028 feet above sea level.

Sound travels 4.5 times faster in water than in air. Whales can hear one another's call hundreds of miles away.

More about underwater mountains (p.36); ocean ridges (pp.10, 11)

The open ocean

The wide ocean

Oceans cover 71 percent of the Earth's surface — over 137 million square miles. The average depth of the oceans is approximately 13,000 feet, and the total volume of water is about 330 million cubic miles. There are five major oceans in the world — the Atlantic, Pacific, Indian, Arctic and Antarctic oceans. They are all connected, and water flows between them in currents at various depths.

The blue sea

Water absorbs light, so the deeper in the sea you go, the darker it gets. In fact, most of the great volume of the ocean is dark. No light reaches below 3,300 feet. In the upper waters, the color of the light changes as you go deeper. This is because the water absorbs red light much more than blue light. So in deep water, only blue light remains, and the scenery appears blue.

If you shine a flashlight at this depth, bright colors appear. This is because the color of an object is due to the color of light that it reflects. A red object will appear red only if it reflects red light. If there is no red light, it will appear black.

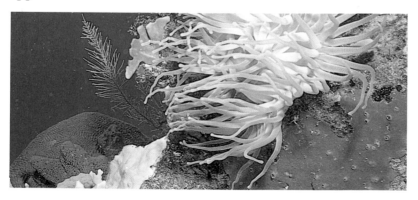

Flashlight fish

In the deep sea it is so dark that many animals produce their own light. Some have luminous lures which they wiggle to attract prey. Others have patterns of light dots along their flanks to help them recognize their mates.

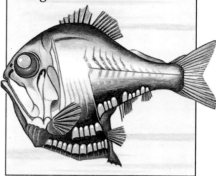

Treasure trove

Almost every known element is found in the ocean. For every 2,200 pounds of seawater there are, on average, 66 pounds of sodium chloride (common salt), and 11 pounds of other salts. Many elements are present in minute quantities – copper, lead, nickel, cobalt, even gold. The total amount of gold in the sea is more than 1,000 times all the gold in Man's possession. There are probably over 14 million tons of silver in the sea, but you would have to strain nearly 2,000 gallons of seawater to find just one grain of silver.

Living under pressure

The weight of the water creates great pressures in the ocean. Pressure increases the deeper you go. In the deepest part of the ocean, the water presses more than a thousand times harder than is does at the surface. This would be like ten full-grown elephants sitting on top of you.

The salt sea

The amount of salt in seawater is called its salinity. Salinity varies from place to place according to how much fresh water is coming in from rivers, how much rainfall there is over the oceans, and how fast the water is evaporating at the surface. When the Sun evaporates the water, the salt becomes concentrated.

The cool deeps

As you go deeper in the ocean, farther from the warmth of the Sun's rays, the water gets colder. In deep water the temperature may be only 35°F. At the surface it varies from over 85°F in the tropics, to 28.4°F in polar waters.

Seawater freezes at 28.4°F. In polar regions, part of the ocean is permanently frozen, and part of it freezes in winter and thaws in summer. Here, up to six feet of ice can form in winter. In summer, when the pack ice over the sea melts, it breaks up to form flat islands of ice. Icebergs also break away from melting glaciers and drift toward warmer latitudes, often traveling thousands of miles before melting in the warmer seas. Icebergs can be hundreds of miles long and hundreds of feet high.

▲ Flat topped icebergs are found in the Antarctic.

▲ Salt is produced by evaporating seawater in shallow pools.

Did you know?

Eskimos use sea ice as a source of fresh water for drinking. This is because when the surface of the sea freezes, the salt is left behind in the water.

Only about one eighth of an iceberg shows above the surface of the sea. The part below the water may be even wider than the part you can see. This makes icebergs a threat to ships.

More about light and color (pp. 90, 91); pressure (p. 119)

Wind, waves and tides

Tides

Along the coast, the edge of the sea comes farther up the land at certain times of the day. This is due to the tides. In most places there are two high tides every 24 hours and 50 minutes. After high tide, the water retreats (ebbs) a certain distance before returning.

▲ High tide in Fiji.　　　　▼ Low tide in Fiji.

The tides are really giant waves due to gravity. They are caused by the gravitational pull of the Moon, and to a lesser extent, the Sun. Water is fluid, so it can move in response to gravity. When a particular part of the Earth is in line with the Moon, the water bulges out and the tide rises. As the Earth spins on its axis, this bulge moves across the oceans like a giant wave.

At the opposite side of the Earth, there is a similar bulge. This is due to an opposite force, called centripetal force. You can experience this if you try swinging a bucket of water around your body. Even though the bucket is tilted, the water does not fall out. It is pushed against the bucket by centripetal force.

Spring and neap tides

When both the Moon and the Sun are in line with the Earth, at new moon and full moon, the tides are at their highest, and are called spring tides.

spring tides

new moon

full moon

At quarter and three-quarter moon, the Sun and Moon are at right angles, so the gravitational pull of the Moon is partly canceled out by the gravitational pull of the Sun, and the tides are at their lowest. We call these neap tides.

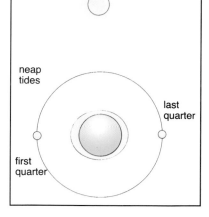

neap tides

last quarter

first quarter

Wind and waves

When wind blows over the surface of water, it sets up waves. As soon as there is the slightest unevenness in the water surface, the wind pushes against the up-slopes, making the waves higher. The longer the wind blows, the stronger it is, and the greater the distance over which the wind is acting, the higher the waves, and the longer the distance between their crests. These long-distance swells, sometimes with hundreds of feet between their crests, can travel for thousands of miles. Rough seas can suddenly appear when the sky is clear and blue, having been produced by a storm far out to sea.

When a wave reaches shallow water, it is slowed down by friction with the seabed. The distance between the wave crests decreases, and the wave height increases, as the water at the top of each wave overtakes the water at the bottom, and topples forward to form a breaker.

Waves

A boat floating on the waves does not move forward; it simply bobs up and down. This is because the water in a wave does not actually travel forward. Each water particle travels in a circle, up and forward on the wave crest, down and back as the wave passes.

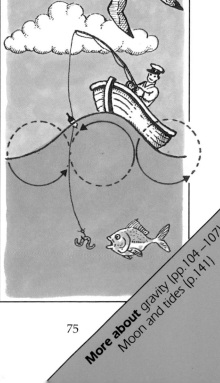

Fifty-foot tides

The height of the tide varies with the shape of the sea bed and the coastline. In some places, like the Bay of Fundy in Canada, and parts of the British Isles, the tide may rise and fall 50 feet a day. In others, like Hawaii, the rise and fall is only 1 to 2 feet.

More about gravity (pp.104–107); Moon and tides (p.141)

Water on the move

The ever-moving oceans

The oceans contain about 330 million cubic miles of water, all of it in permanent motion. Winds, waves, tides and currents help to move the water at all depths.

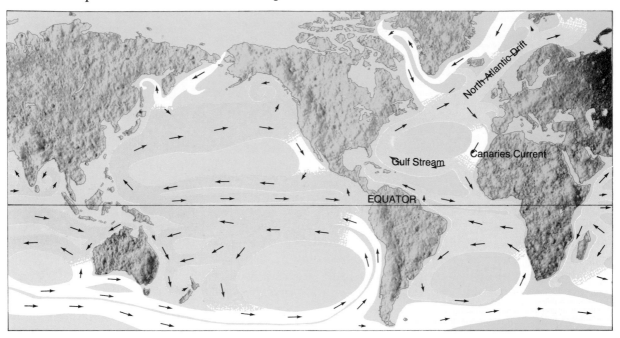

▼ Warm currents (pink) and cold currents (blue) form great revolving gyres in the world's oceans.

Currents

Waves and tides do not move water far, but currents do. When winds blow for long periods in the same direction, they set up great surface currents like the Gulf Stream, which flows up the east coast of the United States, crosses the Atlantic Ocean and continues up the west coast of the British Isles and northwest Europe.

The current does not follow the exact path of the wind. This is because of the Coriolis effect, which is due to the spinning of the Earth on its axis. This makes currents turn to the right in the northern hemisphere, and to the left in the southern hemisphere. As you can see, the ocean currents follow great circles, called gyres.

The Gulf Stream

The Gulf Stream is a warm water current, 37 miles wide and more than 2,000 feet deep. In places it flows at a rate of 100 miles a day. It travels northeast up the coasts of Central and North America, then slows down, spreads south and splits into the North Atlantic Drift and the Canaries Current.

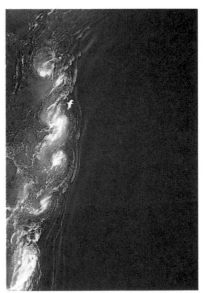

▲ Where two masses of water meet, swirling eddies mix the water along between them.

Deep creeping water

There are also currents flowing deep in the ocean. These are due to movements of water masses of different temperatures or salt contents. Cold water is denser than warm water, and tends to sink. It takes with it a lot of oxygen dissolved from the atmosphere, and is an important source of oxygen for deep water animals. At the poles, cold water from the melting ice sinks to the ocean floor, and travels toward the equator at great depths.

▲ Antarctic pack ice starts to melt.

Very salty water is heavier than less salty water, and also tends to sink. At middle levels in the ocean, masses of warmer, salty water move between the surface currents and the deep water currents. One of these currents comes from the Mediterranean Sea, from which very salty water escapes into the Atlantic Ocean through the Straits of Gibraltar.

Water and the weather

Ocean currents have a big effect on climate. These palm trees are on the Isles of Scilly which are about 50 degrees north of the equator, off the coast of England. The islands are warmed by the Gulf Stream.

Much of our rainfall comes from winds that blow across the sea, pick up moisture from it, then deposit it as rain over the land. Where cold currents flow along the coast, the air is cooled and cannot pick up much water. Near-by land, such as the coast of Peru, gets so little rain that it remains a desert.

Food from the deep

The remains of plants and animals that sink to the ocean floor decay, releasing nutrients. Where currents carry large volumes of water away from the land, water wells up from the ocean deeps to replace it. This water is cool, but rich in nutrients for the marine animals and plants that live along these coasts. Such coasts, like the shores of Peru and West Africa, have great fishing industries.

Did you know?

The Sargasso Sea, a huge revolving mass of water and seaweed in the mid-Atlantic, is the largest whirlpool in the world.

Very cold water from the North Pole is carried by deep water currents all the way to the Pacific Ocean.

Some of the ocean's water moves so slowly that it will be thousands of years before it reaches the surface.

More about Coriolis effect (p.79); salinity (pp.73, 126)

The Earth's atmosphere

A blanket of air

The Earth is surrounded by a layer of air called the atmosphere. The atmosphere is made up of a number of different gases, present in different amounts. The most common gas is nitrogen, and it makes up about 78 percent of the air we breathe. The next most common gas is oxygen. It forms nearly 21 percent of the atmosphere. All living things need oxygen to carry out their life processes. Carbon dioxide is present in much smaller amounts. Only .03 percent of the air we breathe contains carbon dioxide, but it is very important. Plants use it to make food during photosynthesis. There are minute amounts of other gases in the atmosphere. These are the rare gases such as helium, krypton and xenon. The atmosphere also contains water vapor, which is the gaseous form of water.

▲ The atmosphere protects the Earth's surface by filtering out the harmful radiation from the Sun. It also insulates the Earth and stops the Sun's heat escaping back into space once it has warmed the Earth's surface.

PUZZLE ?
What prevents the Earth's atmosphere from floating off into space?
Answer on page 151.

The atmosphere is made of three main layers – the ionosphere, stratosphere and troposphere.

The ionosphere extends about 50 miles above the Earth's surface. Here there is very little air — the air is rarefied. The temperature of the ionosphere gradually rises as you move away from the Earth.

The stratosphere extends about 30 miles above the Earth's surface. It contains very little air or water vapor. It is colder than the ionosphere, but warmer than the troposphere. Its highest temperature is about 32°F.

Ozone is a gas formed by the effect of the Sun's ultraviolet radiation on oxygen. It is important because it stops most of the Sun's ultraviolet radiation reaching the Earth. Ozone occurs in the lower layers of the stratosphere.

The troposphere is the bottom layer of the atmosphere. It is about 10 miles thick and it contains nearly all the atmosphere's air, water vapor and water droplets, or clouds. The temperature of the troposphere gradually drops until it reaches the stratosphere.

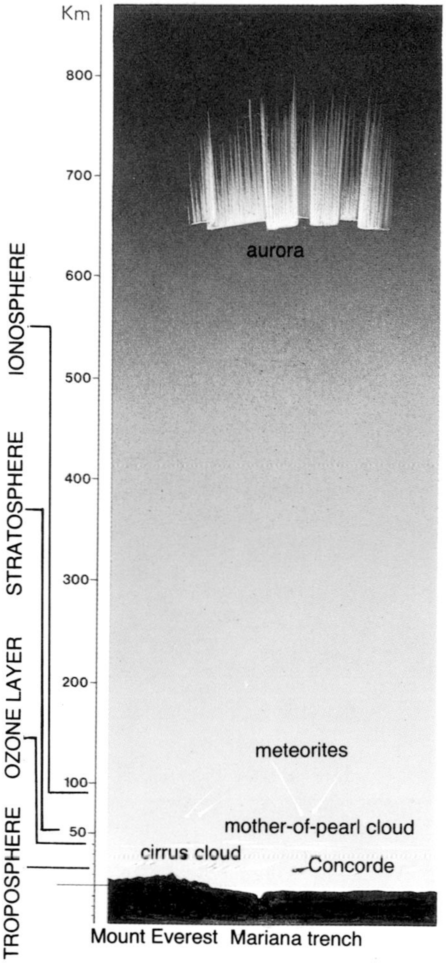
Km
800
700
600
500
400
300
200
100
50
aurora
meteorites
mother-of-pearl cloud
cirrus cloud
Concorde
Mount Everest
Mariana trench
IONOSPHERE
STRATOSPHERE
OZONE LAYER
TROPOSPHERE

Air pressure and wind

Warm air is lighter and less dense than cold air. Because of this, it rises up into the atmosphere. As it does this, it leaves behind an area of low pressure. This is because the air molecules are no longer pressing down so heavily on the Earth's surface. Cold air presses down heavily on the Earth's surface and creates the opposite effect of warm air. It produces areas of high pressure.

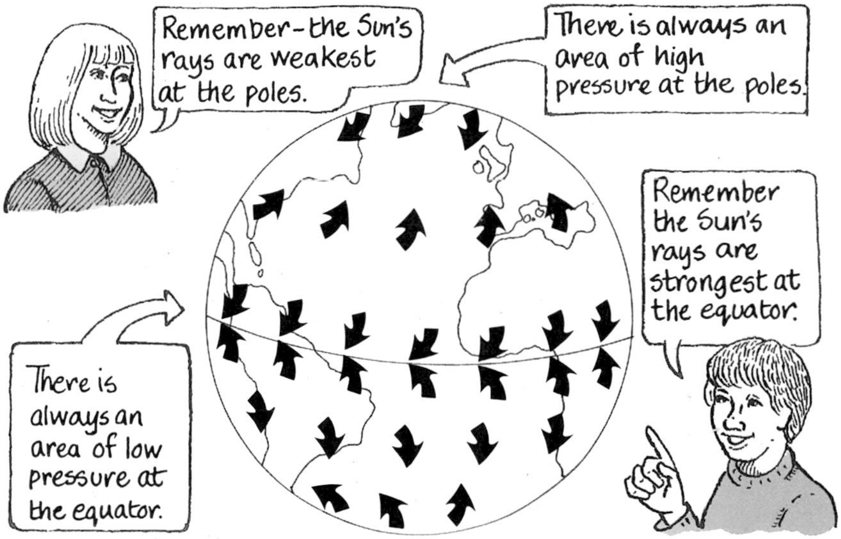
Remember-the Sun's rays are weakest at the poles.
There is always an area of high pressure at the poles.
Remember the Sun's rays are strongest at the equator.
There is always an area of low pressure at the equator.

Winds which blow over the Earth's surface are caused by areas of high and low pressure. A gas always tries to move from high to low pressure, so winds blow from high to low.

Air has weight which we call air pressure. Air pressure is different on different parts of the Earth's surface. It is greatest at sea level because the full weight of the atmosphere is pressing down. The higher up you go in the atmosphere, the less air there is. At 60,000 feet above sea level, the air pressure is about one-tenth of that at sea level.

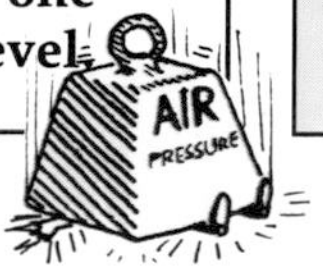
AIR
PRESSURE

The Coriolis effect

Winds which blow over the Earth's surface never blow in straight lines. Because of the Earth's rotation, winds blowing in the northern hemisphere are bent to the right. In the southern hemisphere, winds are bent to the left. This bending of the winds because of the Earth's movement is called the Coriolis effect.

Did you know?

The weight of the Earth's atmosphere is about 5.5 billion tons.

The weight of air in an empty tumbler is equal to the weight of an aspirin tablet.

High winds, called jet streams, blow between the troposphere and stratosphere. They reach speeds of 200 mph.

More about ozone (pp.97, 129); aurora (p.143)

Clouds

Different types of clouds

If you look at a photograph of planet Earth taken from space, it looks like a huge, blue ball covered with areas of white. These white patches are either clouds or regions of snow and ice. Most clouds contain microscopic droplets of water, but some are made up of tiny ice crystals. There are a number of different types of cloud, and scientists classify them by shape and appearance. Here are pictures and descriptions of the three main types of cloud.

A

Cirrus clouds appear as thin, curly and wispy shapes surrounded by blue sky. They are formed in the upper troposphere and contain ice crystals. .

B

Cumulus clouds appear as heaped-up clusters like loose balls of cotton. They are the typical clouds of a summer's day. They have flat bases and dome-shaped tops, and they sometimes build up into thunderclouds.

C

Stratus clouds are formed when cumulus clouds group together to form a continuous layer. Stratus clouds are usually much grayer in color than cumulus clouds and they are the typical clouds of a wintery November day. The bottom of the stratus layer is usually about 1,600 feet above the ground, in the lower troposphere.

Cloud formation

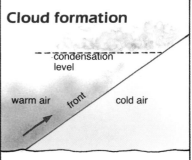

When warm air meets a band of cold air, the warm air is pushed upward. Its water vapor condenses to water droplets when it reaches the condensation level. This forms clouds.

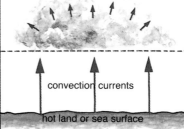

Warm air rises when the ground or sea is heated. Again the water vapor it contains condenses to form clouds.

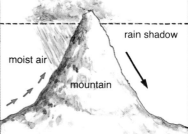

Wind blowing against the sides of mountains is forced upward. The water vapor in the air condenses higher up in the atmosphere to form clouds.

Remember different types of cloud can combine to form other types of cloud. There are about ten different varieties of cloud.

Clouds and change

Cloud formation is all part of the Earth's changing weather pattern. Clouds are produced by masses of warm air rising. As warm air rises, it leaves behind areas of low atmospheric pressure beneath it. These low pressure areas are called depressions. Cold air has the opposite effect. Cold air is heavier than warm air, and it sinks down to the Earth's surface. This creates an area of high pressure, which scientists call an anticyclone. These centers are moving about continuously. It is these changes of clouds and high and low pressure areas which give the Earth its different and changing weather patterns.

▲ A cumulonimbus cloud. If you were on the ground, you would experience a thunderstorm. But in an airplane, flying above the cloud, the weather would still be clear and fine.

The life of a cumulus cloud

Sometimes cumulus clouds get bigger and bigger as they receive masses of rising warm air. The hot air seems to "feed" the cumulus clouds. The clouds grow in size until they reach a height of about 33,000 feet above the ground. The accumulation of cumulus clouds form cumulonimbus clouds, or thunderclouds. These clouds are full of energy in which electrical charges build up and high winds develop. The upper part of a cumulonimbus cloud develops a positive electrical charge, and the lower part a negative electrical charge. Eventually these electrical charges are released and flashes of lightning are produced and sent down toward the Earth's surface.

Flying through clouds

If you have ever flown in an airplane, you will have certainly flown through clouds. Your most dramatic experience may have been during the plane's descent, just before landing. At this time, the bright sunshine is suddenly cut out as you enter the layer of stratus cloud about 3,000 feet above the ground. The plane also bumps about in this kind of cloud. Can you think why? Find out on page 151. Once you have come out from under the stratus cloud, you can see the ground below, and the plane lands shortly after.

Did you know?

The winds which develop inside cumulonimbus clouds may reach speeds of 125 mph.

Small, pink "mother-of-pearl" clouds form as high as 20 miles in the atmosphere.

Clouds above the Scottish Highlands have been seen in the city of Bath, 400 miles away.

More about weather (pp.82, 83); thunderclouds (p.93)

The weather

Weather systems

There are two main types of weather system and they both depend on air pressure. Cold air sinks downward to the Earth's surface. This causes a high pressure weather system. Warm air moves upward from the Earth's surface. This brings about a low pressure weather system. The centers of high pressure weather systems are called anticyclones. Those of low pressure weather systems are called depressions. Weather systems are moving and changing all the time, and it is this which causes the different types of weather.

Weather fronts

Where a depression system meets an anticyclone, a weather front is formed. A front is the dividing line between the cold air of a depression and the warm, moist air of an anticyclone.

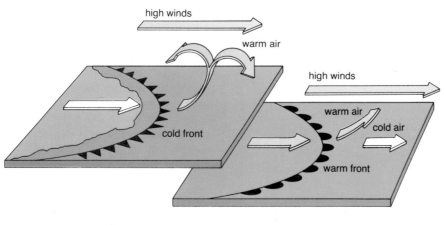

high winds
warm air
high winds
cold front
warm air
cold air
warm front

When cold air meets warm air, a cold front is formed. The warm air is pushed upward.

When warm air meets cold air, a warm front is formed. Again the warm air rises.

The Earth's axis is tilted. As the Earth moves round the Sun, the amount of radiation from the Sun reaching different parts of the Earth's surface varies. These variations cause movements in the Earth's prevailing winds. They also bring about the different seasons north and south of the equator.

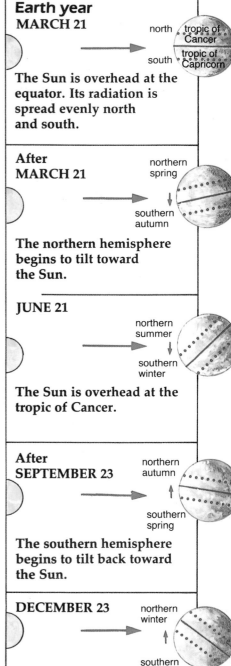

Earth year
MARCH 21

north · tropic of Cancer
south · tropic of Capricorn

The Sun is overhead at the equator. Its radiation is spread evenly north and south.

After MARCH 21

northern spring
southern autumn

The northern hemisphere begins to tilt toward the Sun.

JUNE 21

northern summer
southern winter

The Sun is overhead at the tropic of Cancer.

After SEPTEMBER 23

northern autumn
southern spring

The southern hemisphere begins to tilt back toward the Sun.

DECEMBER 23

northern winter
southern summer

The Sun is overhead at the tropic of Capricorn.

Seasonal air masses and monsoons

The air masses which develop over the world's oceans are different from those which develop over the continents. Because of these different kinds of air, coastal regions often have very changeable weather. This is because the two types of air masses meet at the coasts, where oceans and land come together. These areas are called transition zones. Changes in the seasons sometimes bring about changes in the direction in which certain winds blow. In Southeast Asia in winter, a high pressure weather system develops over the land. Winds blow away from the high pressure zone. These are the trade winds. In summer, the Sun's radiation heats up the air and a low pressure zone is created. Now the trade winds are reversed and they blow inland from the ocean, bringing moisture and heavy rain. These are the monsoons.

Weather forecasting

Weather stations are found all over the world, both on land and at sea. Scientists in weather stations measure a number of things in the air. Balloons filled with hydrogen are sent into the upper atmosphere to record conditions there. All the information a balloon collects is transmitted back to the weather station, where meteorologists (scientists who study weather) analyze it.

Weather satellites

Weather satellites orbit the Earth and send back pictures showing changing cloud patterns. Satellites also track the movements of hurricanes and collect data about winds, humidity and temperature in the upper atmosphere.

Weather stations pass their information to weather centres.

Weather maps

Weather stations send their data to weather centers. The data is fed into computers, and weather maps are produced. The maps have patterns of lines drawn on them, which show the weather systems, weather fronts (like the one in the picture above) and areas of low and high pressure. Meteorologists use the information to predict how the weather will change.

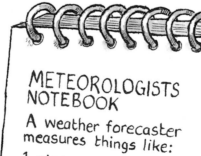

METEOROLOGISTS NOTEBOOK

A weather forecaster measures things like:
1. air pressure
2. temperature
3. humidity (moisture)
4. wind speeds and directions
5. precipitation (rain, hail, snow, sleet, fog)
6. cloud types and their heights.
7. visibility

Did you know?

Satellites measure wind speeds at sea level by observing the movement of buoys floating at sea.

Weather forecasting really developed only after 1844. This was when Samuel Morse invented the electric telegraph machine.

More about air pressure and wind (pp. 79, 81); monsoons (p.87)

Freak weather

Nearly half the Earths' surface lies between the latitudes 30°N and 30°S. Most of this is tropical and subtropical.

Headings like this appear in international newspapers every year. The reports are usually about events taking place in tropical and subtropical parts of the world, but they cause great interest wherever the news is read. Hurricanes, cyclones and typhoons are very similar. They are the names given to spectacular and powerful tropical storms, which are called hurricanes when they take place in the west Atlantic Ocean, cyclones in the Indian Ocean and typhoons in the Pacific Ocean. Tropical cyclones can be dangerous, and some of them cause great damage and loss of life.

Cyclones

Cyclones are low pressure weather systems with very strong winds circling round the low pressure center. Some cyclones may be 300 miles in diameter, with winds blowing at more than 125mph. All cyclones start off above warm tropical seas. Here the Sun's radiation causes vast amounts of evaporation to take place from the surface of the oceans. As the water vapor rises up, huge amounts of energy are transferred from the sea to the atmosphere. This produces a series of thunderstorms. It is from some of these that cyclones develop.

Tornadoes are similar, but much smaller, sometimes only a mile or so across from one side to another. But they can be just as powerful, with winds spinning at even higher speeds than those of cyclones.

The tropical parts of the world have special weather systems. Cold air moves continuously from the North and South Poles toward the equator. When the two meet, air from each is pushed upward high into the atmosphere. This air carries enormous amounts of water vapor which condenses to form clouds. The rain falls as tropical rainstorms in a band around the equator.

When is a cyclone a hurricane?

A hurricane is the name given to a cyclone which develops in the western Atlantic Ocean. Some may even start life as a thunderstorm above West Africa. They begin as an area of low pressure which is carried west toward America and the Caribbean islands. Hurricanes get their energy from the warm tropical seas over which they travel. They spin at very high speeds and the winds inside them may blow at more than 125mph.

◄ This is a hurricane photographed from space.

The eye of the hurricane

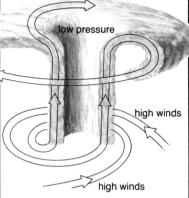

low pressure

high winds

high winds

The center, or eye, of a hurricane is where the air pressure is lowest. It is a calm region which is free from wind, although strong winds blow around the outside of the eye. As the center of a hurricane passes over a part of the Earth, the strong winds from one direction stop suddenly. Then there is a period of calm for two or three hours before the winds start to blow again. This time they blow from the opposite direction.

Tornadoes

A tornado, or twister, is another spinning column of air. Tornadoes are much smaller in diameter than hurricanes. Some of them are only several hundred feet across. However, they develop tremendous wind speeds, often as high as 300 mph. The center of a tornado also has a very low pressure. It is lower than the pressure inside the buildings in its path. The buildings explode like pricked balloons.

Dust devils and waterspouts

In hot desert regions, clouds of sand and dust are sometimes sucked up by twisting currents of air. These small whirlwinds are caused by the heating of the air just above the hot sand. The hot air rises very rapidly and pulls the dust up with it. This creates the spinning column of dust called a dust devil. Sometimes these columns reach a height of 3,300 feet. They tend to move slowly along a narrow path which may be only a 6 feet or so wide. They usually travel at speeds between 3 and 20 mph.

A waterspout is like a tornado, but it occurs over water. The rising air inside carries water up from the surface of an ocean or lake. Most waterspouts are between 15 and 30 feet thick, and between 150 and 300 feet high.

▼ A tornado is a rapidly rotating tunnel of air which reaches downward from a cumulonimbus cloud.

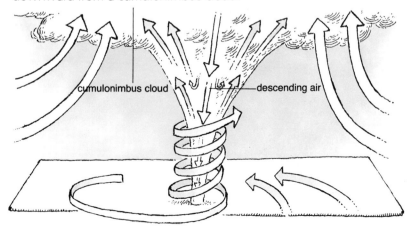

cumulonimbus cloud — descending air

Did you know?

Each year, tropical cyclones cause more loss of life than all other storms combined.

The highest waterspout occurred in 1898 off the coast of Australia. It reached a height of 5,013 feet.

More about wind (pp.52, 53); weather (pp.82, 83)

Climates around the world

What is climate?

When we use the word "climate" we mean the average conditions of sunshine, wind and rainfall which occur in a particular region of the world. Climates vary in different parts of the world. This is because different regions receive different amounts of radiation from the Sun. Some regions are cold, some are hot, and others are in between.

Weather is the daily changes in sunshine, wind and rain.

Climate is the average conditions of sunshine, wind and rain over a long time.

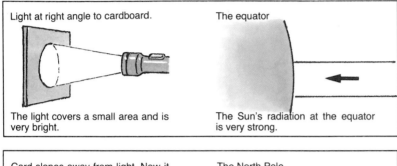

Light at right angle to cardboard.

The light covers a small area and is very bright.

The equator

The Sun's radiation at the equator is very strong.

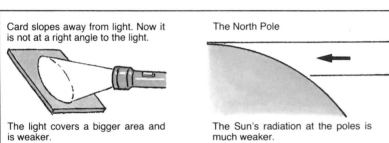

Card slopes away from light. Now it is not at a right angle to the light.

The light covers a bigger area and is weaker.

The North Pole

The Sun's radiation at the poles is much weaker.

◀ A flashlight beam shining on a piece of cardboard makes a small, bright circle of light when it strikes the cardboard at right angles. This is how the Sun's rays shine on the equator, and this is why the equator is hot. The Sun's heat is concentrated. If the cardboard is sloped at an angle, the light patch is oval-shaped and bigger. It is less bright and covers a bigger area. The Sun's rays strike the poles like this. They are less concentrated and do not heat the land as much.

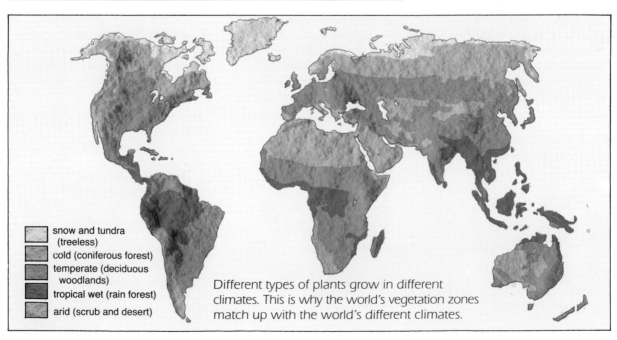

snow and tundra (treeless)

cold (coniferous forest)

temperate (deciduous woodlands)

tropical wet (rain forest)

arid (scrub and desert)

Different types of plants grow in different climates. This is why the world's vegetation zones match up with the world's different climates.

The coldest places on Earth

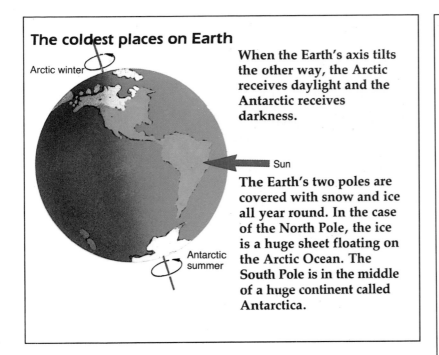

Arctic winter

Sun

Antarctic summer

When the Earth's axis tilts the other way, the Arctic receives daylight and the Antarctic receives darkness.

The Earth's two poles are covered with snow and ice all year round. In the case of the North Pole, the ice is a huge sheet floating on the Arctic Ocean. The South Pole is in the middle of a huge continent called Antarctica.

Currents and mountaintops

Climate is affected by other things apart from latitude. The oceans and their currents can change climates. They can bring both cold and mild climates depending on whether they flow from cold or warm parts of the world.

Climate is also affected by altitude. The farther up a high mountain you climb, the colder it becomes. The types of vegetation also change. Mount Kilimanjaro lies on the equator, and it is the highest mountain in Africa. If you were to climb from the bottom to the top, you would gradually pass through the different zones of climate, starting with the tropical rain forest, and ending up with snow and ice. It would be similar to making a journey from the equator to the North Pole.

Winds of change

Winds also affect climate. Some winds blow in a particular direction at certain times of the year. They are called prevailing winds. The trade winds are important prevailing winds. Some winds carry plenty of moisture. Other winds are dry with not much moisture in them. All the world's great deserts are found in the path of dry winds which bring them very little rain. The moist winds which blow toward India in the northern summer carry plenty of rain. This brings the monsoons.

Wet and dry seasons

Temperate countries have winter and summer seasons. Parts of the Earth in the tropics and subtropics have wet (rainy) and dry seasons instead. The rains always come at a certain time every year, and they are followed by dry weather. The monsoons are the rainy seasons in certain parts of the world.

▶ Mount Kilimanjaro.

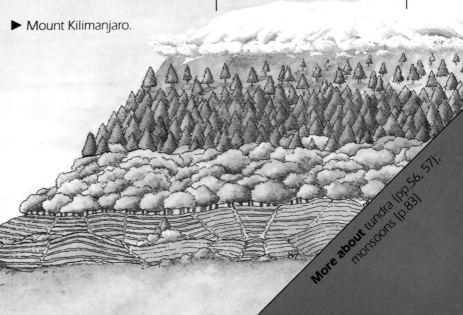

More about tundra (pp.56, 57); monsoons (p.83)

Light

◄ This is a photograph of "earthrise" taken from the surface of the Moon. The Earth is shining because it is reflecting the light from the Sun, which is falling on it. The Sun is the Earth's main source of light and heat.

What is light?

Most things you see do not give off light. They reflect light which comes from some other source. The Moon does not give off its own light. It reflects sunlight. Electric light bulbs give off light, but to do so they have to turn electrical energy into light energy. Some animals and plants can also produce light. In this case, they change chemical energy into light energy.

How does light travel?

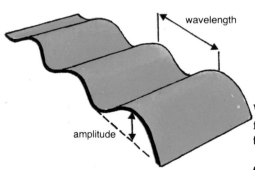

The frequency is the number of waves which pass a certain point every second.

Wavelength is the distance from the top of one wave to the top of the next.

Amplitude is the distance from the bottom of a wave to the top.

Scientists think that light travels in waves, like the ripples on the surface of a pond when a stone is dropped in. Light waves belong to a family of waves called the electromagnetic spectrum. This includes gamma rays, X rays, ultraviolet rays, infrared rays and radio waves. All these waves travel at the same speed. They travel at 186,000 miles per second. Scientists have measured these different waves and found they have different wavelengths. Scientists compare waves by measuring their wavelengths, amplitude and frequency.

From Sun to Earth

It takes the light waves from the Sun just over eight minutes to reach the Earth's surface. The waves travel through the vacuum of space. Unlike sound waves, light waves do not need air molecules to enable them to travel.

Straight lines

Light travels in straight lines. Remember, waves can still travel in straight lines even though the waves themselves are bent. Think of someone making waves in a piece of rope tied at one end. Because light travels in straight lines, it cannot go round corners. If it meets an object through which it cannot pass, it casts a shadow. The part of the Earth experiencing night is in shadow. This is why it gets dark. The fact that objects cast shadows is proof that light travels in straight lines.

Reflection

If you look at yourself in a mirror, you can see your own reflection. Many things reflect light. All polished surfaces do, but mirrors are the best reflectors. This is because a mirror's surface is extra smooth and shiny. If you bounce a ball against a wall, the ball always bounces back at the same angle at which you threw it. The angle at which it hits the wall is called the angle of incidence. The angle at which it bounces back is called the angle of reflection. Light is reflected in the same way. This is called the law of reflection.

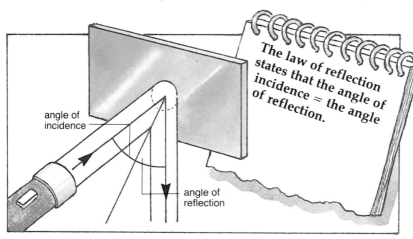

angle of incidence

angle of reflection

The law of reflection states that the angle of incidence = the angle of reflection.

Refraction

Light travels through different materials at different speeds. It travels much faster through air than through water. This is why the spoon in the picture seems to be bent. The direction in which the light is traveling changes at the point where the spoon enters the water. This bending of light is called refraction.

Tricks of light with air

Mirages are "tricks" of light. They occur in different conditions and are sometimes seen in hot deserts and cold polar regions. All mirages are caused by refraction, due to light traveling through air of different densities. On a hot summer's day, air near the ground heats up and becomes less dense. Light rays entering this layer from cooler air above are bent upward away from the Earth's surface. When this happens in desert regions, the thirsty traveler really sees the brightness of the sky shimmering like a lake on the ground. In polar regions, the opposite happens. Cold, dense air lying above the surface of the sea bends the light rays downward. Distant objects, such as ships at sea beyond the horizon, come into view apparently "floating in the sky."

─ *Did you know?* ─

Light travels 42 000 times faster than the Concorde.

In 1798, a mirage occurred at Hastings in England when the whole of the French coast from Calais to Dieppe was seen in the clearest detail. The mirage lasted for three hours. Calais is 62 miles from Hastings.

Distances in the universe are so vast that they are measured in light-years. In one year, light travels 5.9 trillion miles.

More about the electromagnetic spectrum (pp. 96, 97); light energy (pp.110, 111)

A world of many colors

▲ You can see all the colors of the spectrum in this rainbow.

Making white light

Cut a piece of white cardboard in the shape of a circle about 4 inches in diameter. Make a hole in the center big enough for a pencil.

Divide the circle into seven equal-sized segments. Fill in each segment with a different color of the spectrum. Put a pencil through the hole and spin your colored circle like a top.

What happens when you spin your top?

The answer is on page 151.

More than one color

In the year 1666, Sir Isaac Newton made an interesting experiment. He saw a beam of sunlight shining through a hole in his window blind. He allowed the beam to pass through a triangular piece of glass, called a prism. The prism split the light beam up into different bands of color which were thrown on to the wall of Sir Isaac's room. Sir Isaac carried out this experiment several times, and eventually called the colored bands of light a spectrum.

A rainbow is a spectrum

A spectrum occurs naturally when a rainbow is formed. Think what is happening when you see a rainbow. It rains at the same time as the Sun is shining. The raindrops act like millions of tiny prisms. Each one splits the sunlight into its different bands of color. When we look at a rainbow we are really seeing a huge spectrum of the colors red, orange, yellow, green, blue, indigo and violet. These are the seven colors of the spectrum.

Colors have wavelengths

Each color of the spectrum has a different wavelength. The red colors have the longest wavelengths and the blue colors, the shortest. In fact, it is a bit more complicated than this, because each color band consists of a range of wavelengths. For example, the orange band has wavelengths ranging from reddish-orange to yellowish-orange.

Why do we see different colors?

We see only light which is reflected from something else. If you look at a green leaf, you see the color green because the leaf is reflecting back into your eyes the green wavelengths of light. The other wavelengths of light are absorbed by the leaf and you do not see them. This is how we see color. We see only the colors of the spectrum which are reflected by an object into our eyes.

PUZZLE 1

Can you explain what happens when you see a black object?

PUZZLE 2

Can you explain what happens when you see a white object?

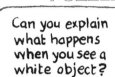

Answers on page 151

Why is the sky blue?

Have you ever wondered why the sky always looks blue or why it appears red during a beautiful sunset? When sunlight enters the Earth's atmosphere, it is reflected by the millions of tiny dust particles and water droplets in the atmosphere. This is called scattering. The shortest wavelengths of light are at the blue end of the spectrum. These wavelengths are scattered more than the other wavelengths. The atmosphere contains enormous numbers of dust particles and water droplets, and these scatter the blue light so much that the sky appears blue.

A red sky at night

At sunset, the Sun is low on the horizon. Its rays have to pass through a much thicker layer of atmosphere than at midday when it was much higher in the sky. As the Sun's rays pass through the thicker atmosphere layer, nearly all the blue wavelengths of light are scattered out. Only the red wavelengths, which are the longest wavelengths in the spectrum, reach your eyes. This is why the sky appears red during a sunset.

Did you know?

Green plants use mainly the red and blue light bands of the spectrum when they absorb sunlight to make their food (photosynthesis).

Only one person in every thousand can see the indigo part of the spectrum.

More about Sir Isaac Newton (p.104); photosynthesis (pp.110, 128)

Electricity

The electric world

Today's world depends upon electrical energy. It is used to light our homes and streets, and to provide power for our factories and communication systems. All our modern technology is based on electrical energy.

What is energy?

In order to understand electricity, we need to look at the building bricks of matter. We need to look at atoms and their structure. Atoms are so small that we cannot see them. The tiniest dust particles that you see floating around your bedroom are each made up of millions of atoms. Even though atoms are so very small, scientists have still been able to find out quite a lot about them and their structure.

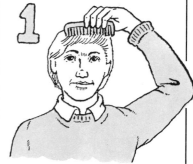

Removing electrons

Removing electrons

Look in the mirror and comb your hair quickly for about 30 seconds.

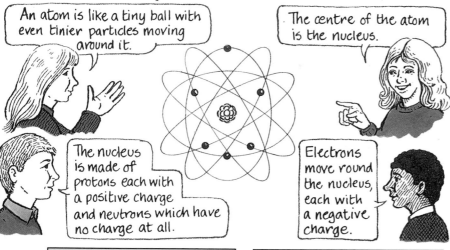

An atom is like a tiny ball with even tinier particles moving around it.

The centre of the atom is the nucleus.

The nucleus is made of protons each with a positive charge and neutrons which have no charge at all.

Electrons move round the nucleus, each with a negative charge.

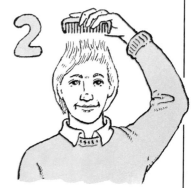

Stop combing and hold the comb just above your hair. You have rubbed some of the electrons off your hair on to the comb.

The comb is now negatively charged and your hair is positively charged. Unlike charges attract, so your hair rises toward the comb.

Repeat step 1 and then touch some small pieces of paper with one end of the comb. Can you explain what happens? Answer on page 151.

Static electricity

When you get undressed, you sometimes hear a slight crackling sound. It often happens when you rub a piece of nylon clothing against another type of material. If you undress in the dark, you sometimes see brief electric flashes like tiny sparks. You are making and seeing static electricity.

Protons and electrons

Normally an atom has equal numbers of protons and electrons. It has equal numbers of positive and negative charges and is electrically neutral. If an electron is removed, the atom has more protons than electrons. It is now positively charged. To remove electrons from atoms, try the simple experiment on this page. It has surprising results.

Current electricity

In static electricity, the electrical charges stay still. There is another kind of electricity, in which the electrical charges keep moving. This is current electricity and it is this kind of electricity we use to send electrical energy from power stations to our homes and factories.

How electricity is carried

You need a good conductor to carry electricity. A good conductor has spare electrons, and these "free" electrons are able to jump from one atom to another. Metals are good conductors of electricity. This is why electric cables contain metal wires. Some materials are bad conductors. They are called insulators. Insulators keep their electrons under control. They have no "free" electrons. Rubber and plastic are bad conductors, but good insulators. They cannot carry an electric current.

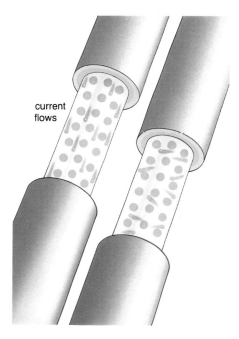

current flows

▲ Copper wire is a good conductor. Normally, the "free" electrons move about randomly, and no current flows. When there are more electrons at one end than the other, "free" electrons are made to move in one direction. This is an electric current.

The Earth's electricity

As the Earth rotates, different parts of its structure spin at different speeds. The molten metal in the outer core lets the mantle and solid crust move faster than the inner core. This works like a giant dynamo, just like the dynamo on your bicycle wheel. As the wheel spins around, it turns the dynamo on the hub and this generates electricity. In the case of the Earth, the electric current is generated within the core. The electric current in the Earth's core produces the Earth's magnetic field.

Lightning

Sometimes clouds become electrically charged. This happens in thunderous weather when cloud particles rub together. Positive charges build up at the top of the cloud and negative charges at the bottom. When a spark of negative charge jumps across the cloud, a flash of sheet lightning is produced.

Sometimes clouds develop extra large electrical charges. An electric current then flows toward the positively charged earth. This appears as a flash of forked lightning.

More about the Earth's magnetic field (pp.108, 109); atoms (pp.116-118)

Heat

James Joule was very interested in turning heat energy into other forms of energy. He wondered about waterfalls and the temperature of the water at the top and bottom. He thought that the water at the top would have a lot of potential energy which would change to kinetic energy when the water fell. When it hit the rocks at the bottom, some of the kinetic energy would be changed into heat energy. One day during their honeymoon, Mr. and Mrs. Joule experimented to test this idea. What do you think they discovered? Answer on page 151.

What is heat?

Heat is another form of energy. It is often produced during other energy changes. For example, when a coal fire burns, the chemical energy stored in the coal is converted to heat and light energy. The heat energy escapes to warm the room. Heat travels in waves, rather like light. Heat also travels at the same speed as light. It takes the Sun's heat waves about eight minutes to travel the 93 million miles between the Sun and the Earth.

Moving molecules

Everything around you is made of tiny particles called atoms. Atoms are too small to be seen, even with the most powerful microscope. Atoms are joined together to form molecules. Even molecules are too small to be seen. Molecules are moving, or vibrating, all the time. This vibration is movement energy, or kinetic energy. When heat waves hit against molecules, the heat is converted into more kinetic energy and the molecules move faster. When substances cool down, their molecules slow down. At very low temperatures, the molecules almost stop moving. The lowest temperature is −459.67°F. At this temperature, the molecules stop moving. They have no heat or kinetic energy. This temperature is called "absolute zero."

Heat energy makes a substance change its state.

The water molecules in ice are held together by strong bonds. Heat breaks these bonds and the ice melts and becomes liquid water.

If even more heat is applied, the water molecules are made to move, or vibrate, even more.

Eventually, the water molecules move so quickly that they become a gas – water vapor. As the gas rises, it cools, or condenses, to form steam.

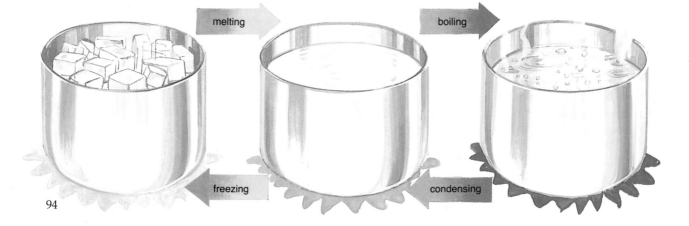

melting

boiling

freezing

condensing

Heat travels in different ways.

Convection

Heat travels in liquids and gases by convection. When a pan of water is heated, the water at the bottom becomes hotter first. The density of hot water is lower than that of cold water. This is because its molecules are moving and vibrating more quickly. Hot water rises in the pan and cold water sinks down.

This is called convection. The same thing happens with hot and cold air.

Conduction

A metal spoon left in a hot cup of hot liquid conducts heat from the cup along its length. The hot liquid heats the molecules in the spoon at one end. These molecules vibrate more quickly. The vibrations are passed from molecule to molecule along the spoon, and the spoon gets hotter.

Radiation

When heat is radiated, it doesn't need molecules to carry it. The Sun's heat radiates to Earth across the vacuum of space, where there are no molecules.

Scientists call heat radiation infrared radiation. It is this invisible radiation which warms the Earth

Through thick and thin

Different parts of the Earth's surface receive different strengths of radiation from the Sun. The Sun's radiation is greatest at the equator and weakest at the two poles. This is because the Sun's rays pass through a greater thickness of atmosphere to reach the poles. The "extra" atmosphere absorbs much of the Sun's heat rays. The Sun's rays are also concentrated into a much smaller area at the equator. This means they can heat up this area more easily.

Remember

Heat is the amount of energy needed to warm an object. It is measured in joules (J). Temperature is a measurement of how hot or cold an object is. It is measured in degrees Fahrenheit (°F).

Expansion and contraction

Matter expands when it is heated. Solids expand only a little, but liquids and gases expand more. In the same way, matter contracts, or gets smaller, when it cools.

Evaporation

Heat causes liquids to evaporate. Water molecules are evaporating all the time from the surface of oceans and lakes. In order for molecules to escape from a liquid, they need extra kinetic energy. They get this from the Sun's rays.

▼ Heat moves away from the Earth's surface by convection currents called thermals. Hot air currents rise upward and cold air is forced down to replace it. This glider is soaring on hot thermals.

95

More about energy (pp.110–115); atoms and molecules (pp.116–118)

Invisible waves

Somewhere over the rainbow

In the popular movie *The Wizard of Oz*, Judy Garland sang a song called "Somewhere over the rainbow." She was singing about a rainbow like the one on page 90, but the song could also have been about the electromagnetic spectrum instead. The rainbow is really the visible spectrum and it is visible because we can see it. It is a collection of seven colors. Light travels in waves and we know that each color of the spectrum is made up of light with a different wavelength. But the spectrum which we can see is only part of the story. There is more beyond it.

The electromagnetic spectrum

Light waves belong to a much bigger family of waves called the electromagnetic spectrum. Light waves are the only members of this family which we can see. All other waves in the electromagnetic spectrum are invisible to our eyes. All waves in the electromagnetic spectrum have one thing in common: they travel at the speed of light, which is 186,000 miles per second. But apart from this, each wave member of the family is different, with a different wavelength. Each affects things in a different way.

Invisible infrared

Are you one of those lazy people who like to change television channels without getting out of your comfortable armchair? If so, you use a remote control device which gives off infrared rays. You cannot see them, but your television is able to pick them up and is coded to change programs when you flash the information. Infrared waves are the same as heat waves. We cannot see them, but we can feel them as heat.

▲ All the Sun's heat radiation travels to the Earth through space as infrared rays. It is these rays which warm the Earth's surface.

short wavelength
gamma rays

X rays

visible light
violet
indigo
blue
green
yellow
orange
red

ultraviolet

special machines detecting gamma rays

infrared

long wavelength

X ray machine

sunbed

photographic film

electric hob

remote control device

radar

microwave oven

television

radio

▲ The electromagnetic spectrum.

96

X marks the spot

In 1895, a German scientist called Wilhelm Roentgen made a discovery he did not really understand. He was the first person to discover X rays, but the discovery puzzled him. He did not know what they were. He called them "X the unknown." We now know that X rays are also part of the electromagnetic spectrum.

TV and radio waves

Radio waves are the longest waves of the electromagnetic spectrum. Some radio waves are more than half a mile long! They are used to send messages and to carry television pictures around the world at the speed of light. Engineers group radio waves into different bands. Each band has its own special use.

Hot meals

Between radio waves and heat waves there is another group of waves called microwaves. These are used in radar, and also for cooking. Perhaps your kitchen at home has a microwave oven. Micro-wave ovens cook very quickly. The waves pass into the food and give it energy. This makes the food get hot quickly.

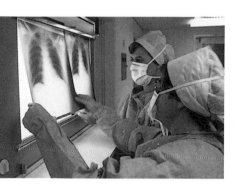

◄ When X rays are fired at your body, most of them pass through quite easily and hit a photographic film placed behind the X-ray machine. The X rays which hit your bones find it more difficult to reach the film because they are absorbed by the bones. Because of this, a shadow is made on the film. When it is developed, an X-ray picture like this one appears.

Gamma rays

The shortest waves in the spectrum are the gamma waves. They come from outer space and from radioactive materials.

Ultraviolet waves can make you sore!

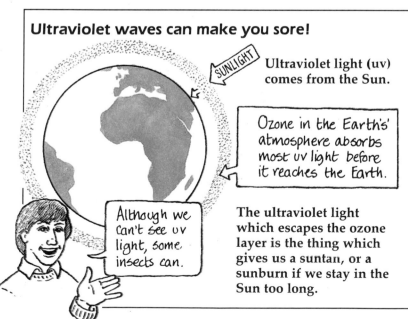

SUNLIGHT

Ultraviolet light (uv) comes from the Sun.

Ozone in the Earths' atmosphere absorbs most uv light before it reaches the Earth.

Although we can't see uv light, some insects can.

The ultraviolet light which escapes the ozone layer is the thing which gives us a suntan, or a sunburn if we stay in the Sun too long.

Did you know?

WASHING POWDER

10 OFF

SPLOSH

WASHES WHITER

Soap manufacturers add a special dye to their washing powders. The dye captures the ultraviolet radiation in daylight or artificial light and makes it become visible. It makes your clothes look even whiter than white!

More about light [pp.88, 89, 90, 91]; gamma and X rays [pp.134, 138]

Sound

What is sound?

Sound is another form of energy. It is produced when an object is made to vibrate. Sound is able to travel only if there are plenty of air molecules around. Air is full of molecules and these can be made to vibrate. They vibrate by moving closer together and then farther apart. Vibrating air molecules make our eardrums vibrate. These vibrations pass to the inner ear, where they are turned into electrical signals which go to the brain. Our brain interprets these signals as sound.

How does sound travel?

When a drum is hit, its skin moves up and down. We say it vibrates. As the skin moves up, the air molecules above it are squashed or compressed. They are pushed closer together. When the skin moves down, the same air molecules are now drawn apart. They expand. When they do this, they compress the air molecules next to them, and so on. The vibrating skin is pushing the air molecules into a pattern of molecules that are first close together and then far apart. Sound waves spread out like ripples on the surface of a pond.

▲ When air molecules are pushed together, it is called compression. When they move farther apart, it is called rarefaction. These bands of compression and rarefaction are the peaks and troughs of each sound wave.

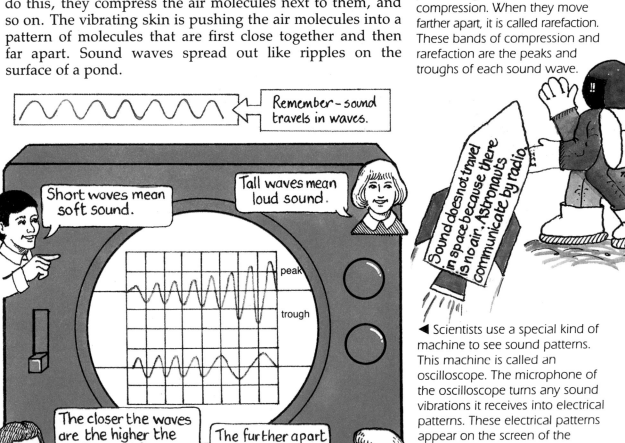

Remember – sound travels in waves.

Short waves mean soft sound.

Tall waves mean loud sound.

peak

trough

The closer the waves are the higher the sound frequency.

The further apart the waves are the lower the sound frequency.

Sound does not travel in space because there is no air. Astronauts communicate by radio.

◀ Scientists use a special kind of machine to see sound patterns. This machine is called an oscilloscope. The microphone of the oscilloscope turns any sound vibrations it receives into electrical patterns. These electrical patterns appear on the screen of the oscilloscope as wave patterns.

The loudness of a sound is measured in units called decibels (dB). Here are some common sounds.

How loud is sound?

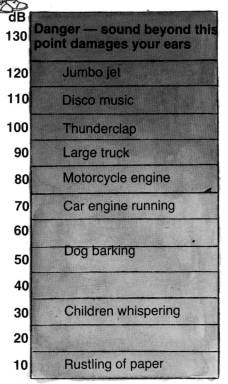

dB	
130	Danger — sound beyond this point damages your ears
120	Jumbo jet
110	Disco music
100	Thunderclap
90	Large truck
80	Motorcycle engine
70	Car engine running
60	
50	Dog barking
40	
30	Children whispering
20	
10	Rustling of paper

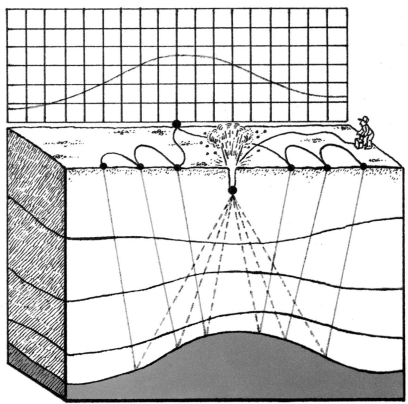

▲ The louder the sound, the higher the number of decibels. A sound above about 130 dB damages your ears. Can you guess what sounds would complete the table above? The answers are on page 151.

▼ Bats use a system called echo-location to catch the insects on which they feed. They produce high frequency sounds which echo back off insects in their flight path. We also use this method (sonar) to measure the depths of the oceans.

▲ Geologists use a seismograph when searching for oil. A small explosion is set off beneath the Earth's surface. Shock waves bounce back from the rocks below. The seismograph records the "echo." This tells the geologists how the rock layers below are arranged.

Did you know?

On August 28, 1883, at 10:00 a.m., the volcanic island of Krakatoa in Indonesia erupted. It produced the loudest noise in recorded history. The explosion was heard 3,000 miles to the west and 2,000 miles to the east.

More about Krakatoa (p.16); waves and frequencies (p.88); seismographs (p.29)

Where on Earth?

Earth grid

It is important to know where you are when you move around. This is especially true when you are traveling long distances over the Earth's surface. You need to know your position and that of other objects. Ships and airplanes need to know exactly where they are at all times. To help them do this, mapmakers draw imaginary lines which crisscross the Earth at regular intervals, like the lines of a graph. They number these lines in degrees. The horizontal lines that run round the Earth parallel to the equator are called lines of latitude. The vertical lines that cross them are called lines of longitude. Navigators calculate the lines of latitude and longitude. By looking at a map and seeing where these lines cross, they can tell exactly where they are anywhere in the world.

Lines of latitude

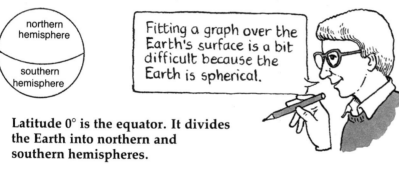

northern hemisphere

southern hemisphere

Fitting a graph over the Earth's surface is a bit difficult because the Earth is spherical.

Latitude 0° is the equator. It divides the Earth into northern and southern hemispheres.

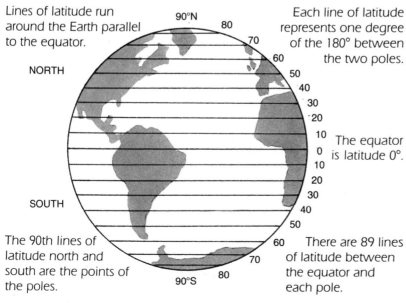

Lines of latitude run around the Earth parallel to the equator.

NORTH

SOUTH

90°N 80 70 60 50 40 30 20 10 0 10 20 30 40 50 60 70 80 90°S

Each line of latitude represents one degree of the 180° between the two poles.

The equator is latitude 0°.

The 90th lines of latitude north and south are the points of the poles.

There are 89 lines of latitude between the equator and each pole.

Lines of longitude

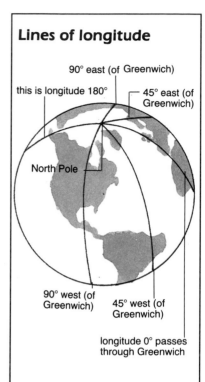

90° east (of Greenwich)

this is longitude 180°

45° east (of Greenwich)

North Pole

90° west (of Greenwich)

45° west (of Greenwich)

longitude 0° passes through Greenwich

Lines of longitude run perpendicular to lines of latitude. Lines of longitude cross the lines of latitude, and because of the Earth's spherical shape, they meet at the poles. Where they cross the equator, each line of longitude is separated by one degree. Longitude 0° passes through Greenwich, London. There is one line of longitude for each of the 180° east and west of Greenwich.

East or west always means east or west of Greenwich.

It's fairly easy finding your way on land. All you need is a map and a compass.

Navigation

Finding your way about is called navigation. Sometimes we navigate over quite short distances and sometimes over much longer distances. Ships and airplanes navigate from one side of the world to the other. Astronauts even navigate beyond the Earth's atmosphere and as far as the Moon.

Navigating at sea

Until recently, navigators on ships used an instrument called a sextant to help them work out the ship's position in relation to the lines of latitude and longitude. They also used a magnetic compass to tell them where the magnetic north was. Nowadays, all modern ships are fitted with a gyroscopic compass. It is a special compass which does not rely on the Earth's magnetic field. Many modern ships are also fitted with electronic equipment which allows them to use satellites in orbit round the Earth to help them fix their position.

Navigation in air

Airplanes use traditional methods of navigation for plotting their course and for fixing their position. They also use complicated electronic equipment — gyroscopic compasses and computers. A system called SHORTAN sends out radar signals from the airplane to beacons on the ground. The signals are returned to the airplane and are used to work out the airplane's position in relation to the Earth's surface. The computers on board make all the necessary calculations to enable the pilot to navigate accurately.

◄ Ships and airplanes use complicated electronic equipment to find their way around the Earth.

Did you know?

Many animals can navigate very accurately. Birds use the Sun and stars to work out latitude and longitude. They carry a map, compass and flight plan in their brains to help them fix their position. It is thought that birds also use the Earth's magnetic field to help them find their way about. Whales do the same thing and so do some insects. Bats even use a kind of radar.

More about tropical latitudes (p.84); longitude (pp.102, 103)

What on Earth's the time?

The Earth spins on its axis counterclockwise. It takes 23 hours and 56 minutes to complete one turn. This turning of the Earth gives us day and night.

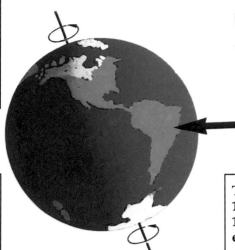

When the northern hemisphere is tilted toward the Sun, the North Pole has 24 hours of daylight every day.

During their winters, the North and South Poles have 24 hours of darkness every day.

The equator always has 12 hours of daylight and 12 hours of darkness every day.

Time zones and GMT

Because the Earth turns continuously on its axis, different parts of the Earth's surface face the Sun at different times. This makes it impossible for all parts of the Earth to keep the same time. Boys and girls set out for school in Australia when children in England are still fast asleep in bed. In 1883, an international conference in London divided the world up into a number of time zones. These zones were based on lines of longitude. Because longitude 0° passes through Greenwich, it was decided to compare all times throughout the world with the time at Greenwich. This is called Greenwich Mean Time, or GMT for short. Different parts of the world are either ahead of GMT or behind it. Each time zone represents 15° of longitude, and each represents a 1-hour change in time.

Sunrise and sunset

Because the Earth spins on its axis counterclockwise, the Sun always rises in the east and sets in the west. It is important to remember this when thinking about time in different parts of the world.

It's easy to work out – the world west of Greenwich is behind GMT.

And the world east of Greenwich is ahead of GMT.

W is the first letter of *west* and the last letter of *slow*. Clocks West of Greenwich are sloW compared to GMT.

F + EAST = FAST. Clocks east of Greenwich are fast compared to GMT.

REMEMBER

The farther east you travel from Greenwich, the earlier the Sun rises compared to GMT. The farther west you go, the later the Sun sets compared to GMT.

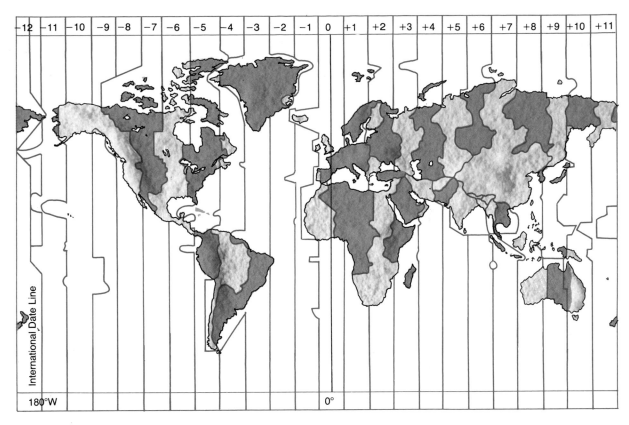

| -12 | -11 | -10 | -9 | -8 | -7 | -6 | -5 | -4 | -3 | -2 | -1 | 0 | +1 | +2 | +3 | +4 | +5 | +6 | +7 | +8 | +9 | +10 | +11 |

180°W   0°

International Date Line

First you lose and then you win

Because the Earth is almost spherical in shape, lines of longitude running east and west of Greenwich meet up at longitude 180° in the middle of the Pacific Ocean. This line of longitude is very interesting because it is rather like a time barrier. It is called the International Date Line. It is the only part of the world where you can gain or lose a day, depending upon which direction you are traveling in.

▲ Each time zone is approximately 15° of longitude, and each time zone represents a 1-hour time change. Lines between different time zones do not run exactly along the lines of longitude. This is because it may not be convenient to divide a country into two time zones.

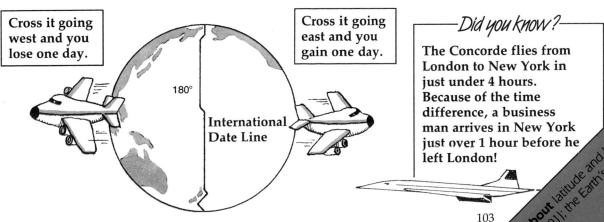

Cross it going west and you lose one day.

Cross it going east and you gain one day.

180°

International Date Line

—Did you know?—

The Concorde flies from London to New York in just under 4 hours. Because of the time difference, a business man arrives in New York just over 1 hour before he left London!

More about latitude and longitude (pp.100, 101); the Earth's shape (p.8)

103

Gravity — why do things fall down?

▲ What will happen when the saw cuts through the branch?

Why does it fall?

The branch falls (and the man with it) because a force is pulling it toward the ground. This force is called gravity.

In the seventeenth century, the English scientist Sir Isaac Newton worked out the theory of gravitation. This says that all particles of matter, from the tiniest part of an atom to the largest star, are attracted to each other. Even today, no one really understands why this is so. We call this force of attraction gravity.

Large objects have stronger powers of attraction than small objects, so smaller objects are pulled toward them. The Earth is very large and heavy, so it has a strong gravitational pull. Therefore, objects fall downward.

How fast does it fall?

If you drop a stone over the side of a tall building, it will travel faster and faster as it falls to the ground — it will accelerate.

You can feel this acceleration for yourself if you push a baby carriage down a steep slope. It becomes more and more difficult to keep up with the carriage.

Jumping on the Moon

The Moon is very much smaller than the Earth, so its pull of gravity is much less. Because of this, when standing on the Moon you would weigh one-sixth of your Earthly weight. This would make jumping very easy.

Things fall faster at the North Pole

Objects fall faster at the poles than they do at the equator. This is because the Earth is not exactly spherical. It bulges at the equator, and is slightly flattened at the poles. This means that objects near the Earth's surface are farther from its center of gravity near the equator than at the poles, so they do not experience such a strong gravitational pull.

How far can you throw a ball?

When you throw a ball into the air, gravity pulls it back down again. If there were no gravity, the ball would simply keep on traveling in a straight line.

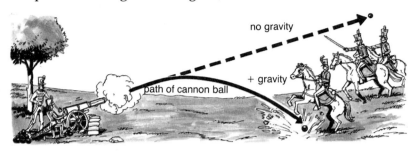

When you throw the ball up, you are exerting a force on it in the opposite direction to the Earth's gravity. A strong man can exert more force than a young boy, so the ball travels farther before falling back to the Earth.

Which falls fastest?

Objects always fall through the air at the same rate, however heavy they are, unless the air resists them to a different extent. The Italian scientist Galileo proved this by dropping a heavy cannon ball and a light musket ball at the same time from a high tower. Both balls hit the ground at the same time.

But if you drop a stone and feather together, the stone will reach the ground long before the feather. This is because the falling object has to push the air aside. The larger the surface area of the object, the more air it has to push aside. This is why the feather falls slower than the stone, and why a man with a parachute falls through the air much more slowly than a man without one.

Weightlessness — zero "g"

Way out in space, astronauts get so far away from the Earth that they experience weightlessness because there is zero gravity. They float in the air inside the spaceship and find it impossible to remain the right way up.

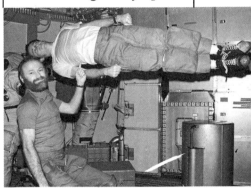

The stone falls faster than the feather.

The parachute slows the fall.

More about Sir Isaac Newton (p.90); the Moon (p.141)

105

Gravity — weight and mass

What do you weigh?

When you use a scale or a spring balance to weigh something, you are really measuring the pull of the Earth's gravity on the object. This pull is greater on objects of large mass than on objects with small mass. Mass is the amount of matter in an object.

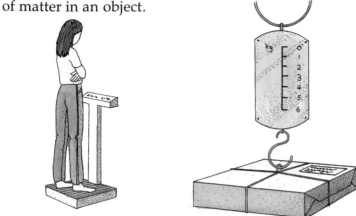

The farther apart two things are, the less strongly they attract each other. The area over which an object can attract another object is called its field of gravity. The strongest pull of gravity is at the center of the object — its center of gravity.

If you weigh yourself in an airplane flying at a high altitude, you will find that you weigh less than you do on the ground. This is because you are farther away from the Earth's center of gravity. Yet you contain just as much matter as you did on the ground. You have the same mass.

Mass is measured using a beam balance (pair of scales). You put the object to be measured on one side and an object of known mass on the other side, and compare the two. Gravity is acting equally on both sides of the balance, so only the mass is being compared.

measuring mass

The plumbline

When you want to build a wall, a simple way of making sure it is vertical is to use a plumbline. This is a weight on the end of a piece of string. Often a lead weight is used, because lead is very dense, so a small piece weighs a great deal. A small stone will work quite well. If you hold the plumbline in your hand, the weight will hang downward toward the ground. In fact, it is pointing toward the Earth's center of gravity.

If plumblines were hung above the Earth's surface in various parts of the world and their paths were continued into the Earth, they would all meet at the center of the Earth. This is because the pull of the Earth's gravity is greatest at its center.

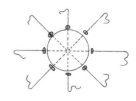

Balancing

When you are standing up straight, your center of gravity is vertically above your feet so gravity acts more or less equally on your whole body. But if you lean too far forward, backward or sideways, you overbalance because your center of gravity is now to one side of your feet.

A tightrope walker can stay on the wire as long as he keeps his center of gravity exactly above the wire. But as soon as he wobbles, the center of gravity moves to one side of the wire so that it is vertically above the empty space. Gravity now pulls the man down on that side making him lean even farther out, until he falls off the wire.

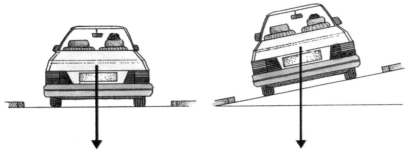

A car going round a sharp corner will not roll over as long as its center of gravity is vertically above the area between its four wheels. But once the center of gravity falls outside the wheels, it becomes unstable.

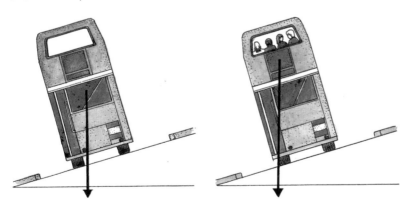

A double-decker bus is taller than a car, and its center of gravity is higher. It is much easier for a bus to become unstable and roll over on a sharp corner. If the bus has more passengers on the top deck than on the bottom, this means there is more mass near the top, and the center of gravity is even higher. The bus is therefore even less stable.

No life without gravity

Without the pull of the Earth's gravity, the atmosphere and the oceans would have drifted off into outer space long ago. There would be no oxygen and no water to support life on Earth.

Did you know?

On the surface of the Earth you are about 3,940 miles from its center.

Without gravity, water would not flow downhill, and rain would not fall to the ground but drift away into space.

A strong field of gravity can bend light rays, and make clocks run slower.

More about gravity (pp.104, 105); matter (p.118)

107

Magnetic Earth

Magnetism and the Earth

The Earth is like a giant magnet with a magnetic field surrounding it. Scientists think that the Earth behaves like this because of its structure and the way different layers spin round. The Earth's core is made of metal, mainly iron. The outer mantle and crust also contain some metallic rocks. The mantle and crust move around at a different speed from the metallic core. As these layers move past each other, they behave like a gigantic generator. This produces electric currents in the core and a magnetic field around the Earth itself.

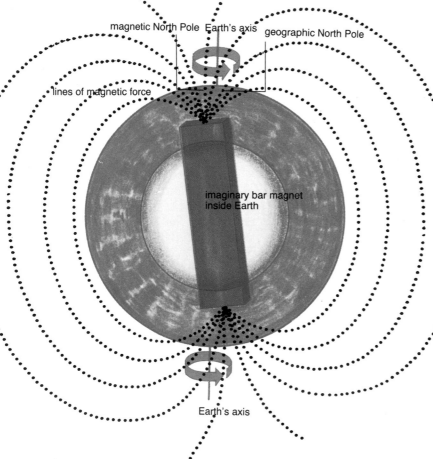

magnetic North Pole   Earth's axis   geographic North Pole

lines of magnetic force

imaginary bar magnet inside Earth

Earth's axis

▲ The Earth has two North Poles and two South Poles. The geographic North and South Poles are the points where the Earth spins on its axis. The other two poles are the Earth's magnetic poles. The Earth's magnetic field is slightly tilted away from its axis on which it spins. This is why the geographic poles are not in the same position as the magnetic poles.

Make a magnetic field
Trace this map of the Earth on a piece of paper.

1

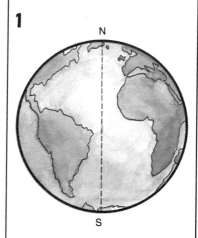

Place your map on top of a small bar magnet. Put the magnet at a slight angle so it doesn't line up with the north-south axis of your map.

2

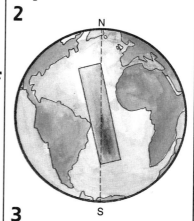

3

Now sprinkle some iron filings over your map and gently tap the paper. Watch how the filings arrange themselves along the Earth's magnetic field.

"Frozen magnetism"

Some rocks have small magnetic particles in them such as iron crystals. As molten rocks cool and become solid, the magnetic particles they contain line up like tiny compass needles. They point to the magnetic North Pole. Rocks like this have the Earth's magnetic field locked into them when they are first formed. They give us a kind of "frozen" record of the Earth's magnetic field and the positions of the magnetic poles at the time the rocks were formed. Scientists call this paleomagnetism (ancient magnetism).

Wandering poles

Scientists have discovered some interesting things about rocks containing iron. For example, in rocks of different ages, the frozen magnetic fields point in different directions. Why should this be? There are two explanations.

The magnetic poles have moved about at different times in the Earth's history.

or

The rocks were in a different place or facing a different direction when they were first formed and have moved since.

Both answers are correct. The Earth's magnetic poles have moved about in the past. In fact, they are still moving an inch or so each year. The continents have also drifted apart so that their rocks no longer face the same way as they did when they were first formed. The magnetic story held in the rocks supports the idea of drifting continents.

Magnetic project

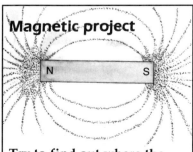

Try to find out where the Earth's magnetic North and South Poles are situated at the moment.

Upside-down magnetism

Scientists have now discovered that the Earth's magnetic field changes in other ways. It becomes weaker and then stronger. When it is at its weakest, the magnetic North and South Poles change positions. We call this polar reversal.

Magnetic travelers

Migrating animals probably use the Earth's magnetic field to help them find their way. Birds can navigate, even in the dark with no moon or stars. Perhaps they use the Earth's magnetic field. Migrating whales probably do the same when traveling from north to south and back again. Even emperor penguins use the Earth's magnetic field to navigate in the darkness of the Antarctic winter.

Did you know?

Compass termites from Australia always build their homes on a north-south axis. Perhaps they use the Earth's magnetic field to help them line up their mounds.

The last-known polar reversal took place about 30,000 years ago.

If you stood still for 24 hours on the geographic North Pole, you would turn around completely once.

More about the Earth's structure (pp. 8 – 11); navigation (p. 101)

Energy

"Energy" is a word we use very often. You have probably seen it on a packet of your favorite breakfast cereals. Everything around us has some energy. But what is energy?

Energy is something which enables work to be done.

Where does the Earth get its energy from?

▼ The Sun is about 93 million miles from Earth. The Earth gets most of its energy from the Sun. About 30 percent of the Sun's energy is reflected back into space by the Earth's atmosphere. The rest passes through the atmosphere and heats and lights up the Earth's surface.

Where do the CRUNCHY POPS get their ENERGY from? Answer on page 151.

Energy capturers

Green plants capture the light energy from the Sun and use it to make sugars. The light energy of the Sun is changed, or converted, to chemical energy. The chemical energy is stored in the sugars made by plants. This process is called photosynthesis. Green plants have a special chemical called chlorophyll to help them do this.

Sun facts

The Sun is the main source of the Earth's energy. The temperature on the surface of the Sun is about 10,500°F. The Sun is 90 percent hydrogen gas. At very high temperatures hydrogen atoms join together to make helium gas. This process produces very large amounts of energy.

110

◀ This coal fire is giving out energy. It gives out light energy, which you can see, and heat energy, which you can feel as warmth. When a coal fire burns fiercely, it also produces sound energy, which you can hear as a crackling noise. Light, heat and sound are all forms of energy. But where did the coal get its energy from in the first place? Answer on page 151.

▲ Geysers are active in volcanic parts of the world. A geyser shoots a column of boiling water high into the air. The water gets its heat energy from deep down in the Earth, where the rocks are very hot. This is an example of geothermal energy.

Burning releases energy

Coal was made from plants which lived nearly 300 million years ago. These plants captured the Sun's energy in their leaves, and converted it to chemical energy which they stored. Over millions of years, the plants were changed into coal. When you light a fire, the coal releases its chemical energy which was stored away millions of years ago. This energy now appears as light and heat energy.

ENERGY FILE

Energy is never made or lost. It is just changed from one kind to another.

Chemical energy — fuel and food contain lots of chemical energy. It is stored energy.

Springs and elastic contain strain energy. It changes to kinetic energy when the spring or elastic is let go.

Even the wind and ocean waves contain energy.

Electrical energy is produced from chemical energy at a power station. Some animals, like electric eels, can also change chemical energy into electrical energy.

Heat is a by-product of other energy changes. It is often wasted energy.

Kinetic energy is movement energy. When you walk, chemical energy in your muscles is changed to movement energy.

Explosions release light, heat and sound energy.

The Sun is our main source of light energy. But light is also given off by other things, including some animals and plants, like fireflies and some fungi.

Everything contains potential energy. If you lift something up, you give it potential energy.

More about energy (pp.112–115); the Sun (pp.142, 143)

Fossil fuels

What are the main fossil fuels?

The main fossil fuels are coal, oil and natural gas. They are called fossil fuels because they were formed from the remains of animals and plants which lived millions of years ago.

Coal

The Earth's coal deposits began to form during the Carboniferous period about 300 million years ago. At this time, the climate was hot and wet, and great areas of tropical swamp covered the Earth's surface. The main plants growing in these steamy swamps were giant horsetails, clubmosses and tree ferns. Relatives of these ancient plants still survive. The coal we use today was produced from the dead remains of these prehistoric plants.

▲ Today's coal deposits started to be formed in Carboniferous swamps.

From peat to anthracite

The plants from which coal was made contained various minerals including carbon. They also contained plenty of water. During the formation of coal, the water was gradually squeezed out and the proportion of carbon was increased. The first substance to be formed was peat. This is a brown material which is made up of about 90 percent water. This was gradually changed to brown coal or lignite, and finally to black coal or anthracite. Anthracite is the best coal. It contains more than 90 percent carbon.

The formation of coal

About 300 million years ago, layers of dead plant material gradually collected in Carboniferous swamps.

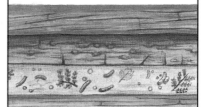

Over millions of years, layers of sand and clay settled on top. The plant remains became squashed, or compressed, by the weight of these sedimentary rocks.

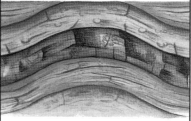

The great pressure from the rocks above gradually changed the plant material into coal. Later, Earth movements pushed the coal layers nearer the surface.

Oil and gas

Oil and natural gas were formed from the dead remains of animals which once lived in the Earth's prehistoric lakes and seas. The formation of oil and natural gas probably began more than 500 million years ago. The animals were all tiny invertebrates which lived in huge numbers in the ancient shallow seas and freshwater lakes.

▲ The oil being loaded on to this tanker will be taken to be refined and then sent to a power station. At the power station, the chemical energy in the oil will be converted into electrical energy and sent to houses and factories to provide their energy needs.

The formation of oil

The remains of millions of tiny animals built up on the floor of prehistoric seas. They formed a layer of thick mud, which gradually got bigger and bigger.

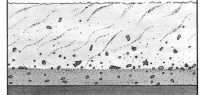

Over millions of years, the dead remains were covered with layers of sedimentary rocks. This compressed them, and changed them to oil and gas. Heat also helped to do this.

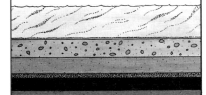

Some oil-bearing rocks are still under the sea. Earth movements have also carried rocks and their oil to places no longer under the sea. Sometimes ancient seas have disappeared, leaving the oil under dry land.

Oil and gas reservoirs

As pressure built up over millions of years, the oil and gas were gradually squeezed out of the rocks in which they were formed. They were carried up by water into porous rocks above. Sometimes the oil oozed out on to the Earth's surface. But in most cases it became trapped in huge underground and undersea reservoirs. It is these which geologists drill into when they find oil.

How much energy comes from fossil fuels?

Oil supplies about one half of the world's energy.

Coal supplies about one third of the world's energy.

Gas supplies about one fifth of the world's energy.

Did you know?

The world's largest oil field is in Saudi Arabia. It covers 3,200 square miles.

The world's largest gas deposit is in Russia. Geologists have estimated it contains 250 million million cubic feet of gas.

The world's coal deposits should last about another 400 years!

Most of the world's gas and oil supplies will run out by the end of this century!

More about Carboniferous period (p.321); peat (p.129)

"Free" energy

There's solar energy or energy from the Sun.

There's a lot of energy in the wind.

What about tidal energy and the energy in the waves?

We are already using hydroelectric energy.

Countries like New Zealand and Iceland are using geothermal energy.

THERE'S ALWAYS NUCLEAR ENERGY! WE ARE USING IT ALREADY.

The energy crisis

You have probably seen newspaper headlines like these before. The world's fossil fuels are being used up much faster than the time taken to produce them. They are getting scarcer all the time. There is still enough coal left for another 400 years. But by the year 2000, most of the world's oil and gas will have been used up. It is important to find new sources of energy. There is plenty of energy around us. We have to learn how to capture and harness it.

Sunny experiments

The original source of most of the world's energy is the Sun. Green plants capture the energy in sunlight, and change it into chemical energy. Now scientists are experimenting with solar energy. They are trying to devise ways of capturing and harnessing it more efficiently.

The radiation from the Sun is 100,000 times greater than the generating capacity of the world's power stations.

▲ This solar furnace produces temperatures of 7,200°F. Its complicated system of mirrors captures the Sun's energy and uses it to melt metals.

◄ Some countries which are short of fossil fuels use water to provide some of their energy. Large hydro-electric dams like this are built to hold back a large volume of water. The water contains potential energy. When it is allowed to flow through a series of turbines, its potential energy is converted into mechanical energy. The mechanical energy is then turned into electrical energy. This can be used in homes and industry.

Turning the tide

Tidal power is produced in a similar way to hydro-electric power. Instead of using running water from a dam, the energy is generated by using the power of the tides. So far, only one tidal power station has been built. This has been placed across the estuary of the River Rance, in France. The energy in the tidal movements is converted to mechanical energy when the water turns a series of turbines. This generates electrical energy.

Waves

Ocean waves hold vast amounts of energy. A big wave in the Atlantic Ocean may be 100 feet high. Imagine how much potential energy such a big wave contains! But scientists find it very difficult to harness this energy. Experiments have taken place to try to capture wave energy, but there is a long way to go.

Geothermal energy

There is an enormous amount of heat energy inside the Earth. Sometimes water which this energy heats up escapes at the surface as hot water geysers, hot springs and steam. Countries like Iceland and New Zealand use hot springs to heat homes and to produce electricity.

NUCLEAR ENERGY

Nuclear energy is produced when atoms of uranium are split. Nuclear power stations are designed to release this kind of energy. Some scientists think nuclear energy is the answer to the world's energy problems. Others are not convinced it is.

Nuclear energy already supplies about two per cent of the world's energy needs

► Winds were first used to make electricity nearly 100 years ago. Now modern windmills are being planned and built to harness wind energy more efficiently. The power in wind depends on its speed. This hurricane is blowing at more than 125 mph. Imagine how much energy it contains!

More about energy [pp.110, 111]; nuclear energy [p.142]

Atoms – the building blocks of matter

What are atoms?

A Greek philosopher called Democritus, who lived in 400 B.C., taught that all substances were made of grains which couldn't be divided. He called these grains atoms, because "atoma" was the Greek word meaning indivisible. Since the time of Democritus, we have gradually learned more about the tiny particles of matter we still call atoms.

Inside an atom

An atom is rather like a miniature solar system. In our solar system the planets are in orbit round the Sun. If you think about it, the solar system is mainly space and atoms are rather like this. They are full of emptiness! At the center of the atom is a nucleus which is made up of two types of particles called protons and neutrons. Each proton has its own positive electrical charge. Neutrons carry no charge. They are electrically neutral. Just as our Sun has the planets traveling round it, so the nucleus of an atom has tiny particles in orbit round it. These are called electrons. Each electron has a negative electrical charge.

Black box experiment

If atoms are so small that we cannot see them, how can we find out what they look like?

You do not have to be able to see an object to work out what it looks like. Try this on your friends. Do not let them see the object you put in the box.

Put a marble in an empty match box and close the box. Make sure the box cannot be opened by sealing it with sticky tape.

Now ask each of your friends to describe the object in the box without opening it.

You will be surprised what they can find out about the object without actually seeing it.

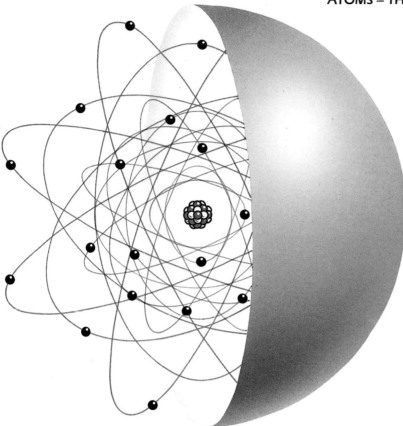

▲ The structure of an atom is like a miniature solar system with the nucleus in the center and the electrons orbiting round it like tiny planets.

Joining together

Atoms join up, or combine, to form structures called molecules. For example, the oxygen in the Earth's atmosphere is in the form of molecules of oxygen. Every oxygen molecule contains two atoms of oxygen joined together. Two-thirds of the Earth's surface is covered with water. This water is made up of water molecules. Each water molecule contains two hydrogen atoms and one oxygen atom joined together. Oxygen combines with many different kinds of atoms. Many of the metals present in the Earth's crust are joined to oxygen. We call them metal oxides.

Different kinds of atoms

Not all atoms are the same in structure. Atoms differ in the number of protons, neutrons and electrons they have. There are more than one hundred different kinds of atoms. Hydrogen is the simplest atom we know. It has only one proton in its nucleus and one electron. The most complicated atom has more than one hundred of each of these particles. Because there are more than one hundred different atoms, there are the same number of elements. An element is a substance made up of atoms of the same kind.

More than one of a kind

Some elements have more than one kind of atom. For example, there are three different kinds of oxygen atom. One of these is the ordinary oxygen atom. The other two are called isotopes. They differ from the ordinary atom in having different numbers of neutrons. Usually substances are made up of mixtures of isotopes. The nuclei of some isotopes give off small amounts of radioactivity.

Did you know?

If all the atoms in the human body were packed together with no space between the nuclei, the pile would be no bigger than a grain of sand!

If the nucleus of a hydrogen atom were drawn the size of a pea, its electron would be at least 980 feet away.

Even to see the biggest atom, it would have to be enlarged more than one million times.

More about atoms and molecules (pp.92, 94, 118); solar system (pp.134, 135, 136, 137)

What's the matter?

Matter is the stuff around us and the stuff which we are made up of. There are three states of matter. These are solid, liquid and gas. Each state of matter has its own particular and special properties. Matter is made up of tiny particles called atoms. Atoms, in turn, join together to form molecules. Molecules join up in different ways to form compounds. It is these different arrangements which give substances their different properties.

The three states of water

An iceberg gradually passes through the three states of matter. Most icebergs break off from glaciers in the Arctic and Antarctic regions. When an iceberg breaks away from its parent glacier, it is a solid — ice. Its molecules are joined together by strong bonds. As it floats into warmer water, some of the molecules gain kinetic energy. They vibrate more and the ice begins to melt and becomes liquid water. Later on, some of these water molecules at the surface of the sea will gain more heat energy from the Sun's radiation. This will make them vibrate even more and they will evaporate. Some of the liquid water will become water vapor.

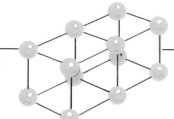

Solids

In solids the molecules are joined together by strong bonds. They vibrate only a little. Solids have a definite shape. They also have a regular crystal shape.

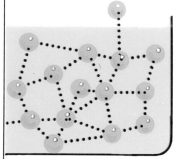

Liquids

In liquids the molecules are close together, but their bonds are weaker. They can vibrate and move more freely. Liquids have a definite volume but no fixed shape. They take up the shape of the container they are put in.

Gases

In a gas the molecules have no bonds between them. They have kinetic energy and move about freely.

Pressure on gases and liquids

You can squeeze a gas into a smaller volume. If you do this, you exert a pressure on the gas. When this happens, the molecules in the gas are squeezed closer together. They become more tightly "packed." If you could exert a big enough pressure, the gas would become a liquid.

You can't squeeze or compress a liquid. The molecules in a liquid are already tightly "packed." They resist any more squeezing or compression. We say that liquids are incompressible.

Solids and pressure

If you apply a big enough pressure to a solid you may change its shape, but you won't change its volume. Can you guess why? Answer on page 151.

Pressure

Pressure is all around us. The pressure acting on a surface depends on the force and area. The greater the force or smaller the area, the greater the pressure. Pressure is measured in newtons per square meter. Molecules in the atmosphere exert a pressure of 100,000 newtons on every square meter of the Earth's surface.

Pressure problem

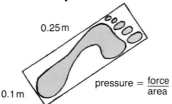

0.25 m

0.1 m

pressure = force / area

Imagine your foot is a rectangle 0.1 × 0.25 meter. Find your weight in newtons. Now work out the pressure your body exerts on the Earth's surface. Remember you have two feet!

Density

Density is how heavy something is compared to its volume. It is an important property of matter. The density of an object is a measure of how tightly "packed" the molecules are in an object. Scientists compare the densities of different objects. They use water as their density standard. Water has a density of 1. All other substances are compared to this.

air 0.0000012   Steel 8   cork 0.2

Floating and sinking

Whether an object floats or not depends on its density compared to water. This is called its relative density. An iceberg floats because its density is less than 1. When an object floats, the weight of water it pushes aside equals its own weight. This is called displacement. A 100,000-ton iceberg displaces 100,000 tons of water.

PUZZLE ?

Steel has a density of 8. It is eight times as dense as water. The world's biggest tanker weighs 621,213 tons. It is made of steel. But it floats! Can you explain how? Think of a ship's shape and how it is built. Answer on page 151.

More about atoms and molecules (pp. 92, 93, 94, 116, 117); relative density (p.130)

Crystal gazing

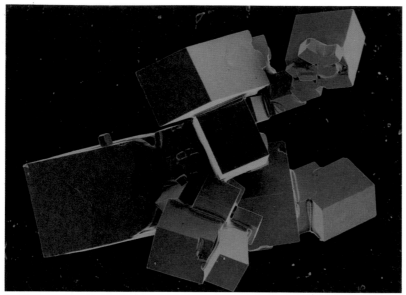

▲ This is a photograph of some crystals of common salt as seen through a microscope. The crystals have been magnified about one hundred times. You can see that each crystal is cube-shaped with flat surfaces and straight edges.

How many sides and how many edges does each salt crystal have?

Find out on page 151.

The shape of crystals

Salt is made up of two types of atoms, sodium and chlorine. This is why the chemical name for salt is sodium chloride. Crystals of sodium chloride are cube-shaped because of the way their atoms are arranged. A single crystal of salt contains thousands of these tiny, cube-shaped units all packed together like miniature boxes. Not all crystals are cube-shaped. In fact, there are seven basic patterns in which crystals develop and these are based on only four common shapes.

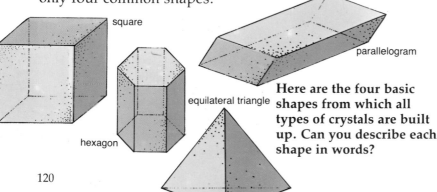

square

parallelogram

equilateral triangle

hexagon

Here are the four basic shapes from which all types of crystals are built up. Can you describe each shape in words?

Growing sugar

Boil a small amount of water in a saucepan.

BE CAREFUL!

When the water has boiled, turn the heat off. Now start adding sugar to the water. Keep doing this until no more sugar dissolves.

When the sugary solution has cooled, pour it into a drinking glass.

Rub a few crystals of sugar on to a piece of damp, thin string or thread and tie one end of it round a pencil.

Hang the string, or thread, in the sugar solution and leave the glass in a cool place for a few days to see what happens.

EAT YOUR RESULTS

Minerals and crystals

Minerals can be identified by their crystal structure and also by their color. Many minerals were originally formed from molten magma. As the rock gradually cooled, the minerals crystallized out. Mica, feldspar, hornblende and quartz, which are found in granite, were all produced like this. The crystals of other minerals were produced in metamorphic rock. These were produced by the action of great heat and pressure. Crystals are often found wedged into cracks in rocks. They got there by being carried in solution in hot water from rocks which were cooling down. Sometimes these crystals are accompanied by metal deposits.

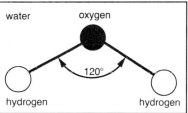

▲ Snowflakes are crystals. All snowflakes are based on the shape of the hexagon but no two snowflakes are exactly the same shape. The hexagonal shape of the snowflake crystal is due to the structure of the water molecules. The angle between each oxygen atom and the two hydrogen atoms which make up a water molecule is 120°. The angles of a hexagon are also 120°.

Identifying crystals

Geologists identify minerals by testing their crystals. They look at shape and they compare weights and densities. They even compare hardness by scratching the surface of the mineral. Crystals vary in hardness and the Mohs' scale produces a hardness table with diamond at the top and talc at the bottom.

Colored crystals

Sometimes crystals are colored by small amounts of other substances. Emeralds are brilliant green because the crystals from which they are made contain traces of chromium oxide. Iron salts give the red color to rubies, and the crystals which make up amethyst contain small amounts of manganese. Minerals such as emeralds, amethysts and rubies are called gemstones.

The hardest crystal

There are many different kinds of minerals. Most of them are mixtures of elements, as like common salt is a mixture of sodium and chlorine. A few minerals are made of only one element. Diamond is a pure form of carbon. Its crystals make diamond the hardest mineral known to geologists.

Did you know?

The world's largest crystal, found in Madagascar, weighed 206 tons.

On the island of Sri Lanka, mica crystals are found which are arranged like the pages of a gigantic book, 6 feet or more across.

The earliest radio receivers made use of galena crystals. This is why they were called crystal sets.

More about gemstones (pp.19, 25); crystals (pp.14, 15)

Water, water everywhere

Two-thirds of the Earth's surface is covered in water.

Water is made up of molecules. Each water molecule contains two hydrogen atoms and one oxygen atom. Water can exist as a liquid, a solid or a gas. At ordinary temperatures it behaves as a liquid. At 32°F it becomes solid ice. At 212°F it changes to water vapor, which is a gas.

Water for life

Scientists have estimated that there are 1.6 million million million quarts of water on the Earth's surface. Water is essential for life, and animals and plants depend on it for many things. Not only do animals and plants take in water, they also give it out. Animals breathe out water vapor and plants lose water through their leaves by a process called transpiration.

Earth log: water

Location	%
Oceans and seas	96.30
Ice and snow	2.19
Fresh water	0.90
Underground water	0.60
In the atmosphere	0.01

This table shows where water is found.

Most of the Earth's water is salt water.

Water roundabout

Water is kept in circulation by the water cycle. The Sun's heat starts the cycle by evaporating water from the land and sea. Gravity brings the moisture back again as rain, hail, sleet and snow. As air is warmed over land and sea, it absorbs water vapor. The moist air rises into the atmosphere and cools. As it cools, the water vapor in the moist air condenses to form clouds. A great deal of water also evaporates into the atmosphere from plants.

▼ When clouds form over the oceans, they are usually driven toward land. If they meet mountains or high ground, they are forced up farther into the atmosphere. This cools them even more and they release their water vapor as rain, snow or hail. This is called precipitation. The water eventually flows back to the sea from the land in streams and rivers. Now the cycle starts all over again.

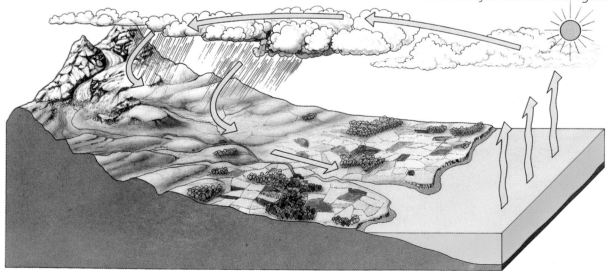

122

Snow white and frost

Sometimes rain clouds rise rapidly through the atmosphere to where the air is freezing. The water droplets turn to hailstones or ice crystals. Ice crystals fall back to Earth as snowflakes. Sometimes the air close to the ground becomes very cold and freezes. In these conditions the water vapor in the air produces ice crystals. These settle on the ground and trees as a thin white layer which we call frost.

A point of dew!

At night the air near the ground is saturated with water. The cold ground may make this condense into water droplets. This happens when the air temperature falls to the "dew point." The water droplets settle on the grass, trees and even structures like spiders' webs. We call this dew.

▲ The Atacama Desert in South America is the driest place on Earth. Parts went without rain for 400 years!

Water and life

Water makes up 65 percent of the bodies of most living things. It is a solvent which dissolves many things. This is why water is so important to animals and plants. Many animals and plants live and reproduce in water. Others have to return to water to breed.

Mists and fogs

When warm, saturated air is cooled, water condenses on dust particles in the atmosphere. This produces water droplets small enough to be carried on air currents. This is how mists and fogs are produced.

—Did you know?—

The Sun evaporates about 1,200,000 cubic miles of water from the surface of the oceans every year.

The continents gain about 9,600 cubic miles of rain or snow every year.

Two-thirds of the Earth's fresh water flows between the banks of the River Amazon in South America.

A human needs at least 260 gallons of drinking water per year.

The kangaroo rat can live its whole life without taking a drink of water.

More about atoms and molecules (pp.116, 117); clouds (pp.80,81)

The world of ice and snow

17TH JANUARY 1912 CAPTAIN SCOTT REACHES SOUTH POLE

4TH JANUARY 1958 SIR EDMUND HILLARY REACHES SOUTH POLE

The regions of the world which surround the North and South Poles are the coldest and most deserted places on Earth. Captain Scott reached the South Pole in January 1912. It wasn't until 46 years later that another explorer, Sir Edmund Hillary, made the same journey. Other scientists have visited the South Pole in recent years, and there is now an American scientific base there. Even so, the polar regions are still very lonely places.

Why are the ice caps so cold?

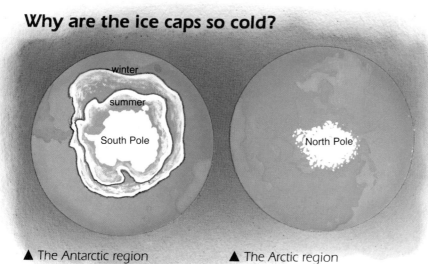

▲ The Antarctic region   ▲ The Arctic region

There are a number of reasons why the two poles are so cold, and you probably know about some of these already. The Sun's rays strike the polar regions at an angle. This spreads the rays out so they have to heat up a much bigger area of land. The warmth from the Sun is, therefore, much weaker at the poles. The polar regions do not move in and out of the sunlight as the Earth spins round. This is because the Earth is tilted. One pole is in daylight while the other is in darkness. There are very few clouds at the poles because there is not much evaporation. The Sun's rays are reflected back into space by the white snow and ice. Because there are no clouds to stop this loss of heat, the polar regions get even colder.

Polar log

The Arctic Ocean is 500 miles across.

Greenland's ice cap is up to 10,000 feet thick.

The South polar ice cap averages 10,000 feet thick.

The largest iceberg ever sighted was recorded in 1956. It covered an area of 11,780 square miles – larger than Belgium.

Artic temperatures vary between 32°F and −40°F.

The average temperature in the Antarctic is −60°F.

◀ The Antarctic region is a vast land continent. The picture shows the area occupied by the pack ice in summer and winter. The Arctic region is an ice sheet floating on the Arctic Sea. The ice cap covers most of the Arctic Sea, and even reaches Greenland, northern Canada and Russia.

Fog banks and sea currents

Cold sea currents from the two poles move toward the equator. On their journey they mix with warmer sea currents. This produces thick fogs which make navigation difficult. Parts of the sea near Newfoundland are covered by fog for nearly half the year.

Volume and expansion

Sea ice normally forms only in the polar regions. Pure water freezes at 32°F. If there are substances dissolved in the water (if it is impure), its freezing point is lowered. Seawater contains salt, which is dissolved in it. The freezing point of seawater is 28.4°F. This is why sea ice does not form very often, except in the world's coldest regions. Unlike most liquids, water expands when it freezes. It takes up a bigger volume. This is why water which has trickled into cracks in rocks gradually splits them. When it freezes, the water expands and gradually makes the cracks wider until the rocks split apart. A similar thing can happen to domestic water pipes in very cold weather.

Density differences

Because water expands when it freezes, ice has a lower density than water. The density of ice is 0.9 grams per cubic centimeter. The density of pure water is 1.0. This is why huge icebergs, weighing many thousands of tons, are able to float. But they only just float. About seven eighths of an iceberg lies hidden under water.

Structure of ice and snow

Ice and snow are both examples of frozen water. Snow forms when rising warm air is cooled quickly. The water vapor forms droplets of water which freeze to produce ice crystals. These fall to the ground as snow. Usually the fallen snow melts when the air temperature rises. But in the coldest parts of the world, the snow never melts. Instead, it gradually builds up layer upon layer. Over thousands of years, the great pressures produced turn the snow to ice, which covers the ground all year round.

◀ Arctic icebergs are usually tall, with an uneven shape. Icebergs from the Antarctic are not so tall, and they are flatter, like gigantic ice tables, with steep, clifflike sides. Can you guess which kind of iceberg this is? Compare it with the picture on page 73. Answer on page 151.

Did you know?

Big Ben would look like this.

The Great Pyramid would look like this.

The Statue of Liberty would look like this.

If the Polar caps melted, the sea level would rise by about 200 feet.

125

More about ice caps (p.46); icebergs (pp.73, 118)

Solutions

Solvents and solutes

If you put some common salt in a glass of water, the salt seems to disappear. We say it dissolves and it produces something we call a solution. The liquid which does the dissolving is called a solvent. The substance which is dissolved is called the solute.

So water is the **solvent** in a salt solution.

And the salt is the **solute** which dissolves.

▼ These limestone caves were formed by a dissolving process. Carbonic acid in rainwater slowly dissolves the limestone.

Chemical weathering is dissolving

Chemical weathering takes place when rainwater seeps through the Earth's rocks and slowly dissolves some of the minerals found there. Rocks such as rock salt are easily dissolved, even in pure water. Other rocks dissolve less easily. Limestone dissolves in rainwater which contains carbon dioxide. The carbon dioxide enters the rainwater as it falls through the atmosphere. The solution formed is called carbonic acid, which is a weak acid. It is this acid which dissolves limestone rocks. Water also reacts with other minerals in a process called hydrolysis. Hydrolysis means "using water to split up." Hydrolysis breaks down certain minerals and turns them into different kinds of substances.

How much, how hot?

The amount of solute which will dissolve in a solvent depends on a number of things. The greater the volume of solvent, the more solute it will dissolve. The temperature of the solvent is also important. The higher the temperature of the solvent, the more solute it is able to dissolve.

Dissolving everything?

In the Middle Ages, there lived a group of early scientists called alchemists. They spent their lives looking for three things. One was finding a way of turning all metals into gold. Another was looking for something which made people live for ever. And a third was searching for something they called the universal solvent. This was something they hoped would dissolve anything and everything.

BUT DIDN'T THEY HAVE A PROBLEM!

What would the alchemists use to store their universal solvent in, if ever they discovered it!

The Earth's vast solution

Two thirds of the Earth's surface is covered by a very complicated solution. It is the salt water of the seas and oceans. Seawater contains, dissolved in it, seventy-three of the elements found in the Earth's crust. It also contains dissolved gases such as oxygen and nitrogen. The most common elements in salt water are sodium and chlorine. These two make up more than 85 percent of the elements found in seawater. Rivers and lakes contain fewer dissolved substances than the seas and oceans. The water in them is generally of a much weaker solution and we call it fresh water.

Salty and even saltier

The amount of dissolved substances in seawater is called its salinity. Salinity is really a measure of saltiness. The average amount of dissolved materials in seawater is about 3 percent. But some seas have less than this and some seas have much more. The concentration of dissolved materials affects the density of water. The stronger the solution, the denser it is. Even different seas and oceans have different densities. For example, the Red Sea is much denser than the Baltic Sea because it contains more salt. Seawater is denser than fresh water.

—*Did you know?*—

A fish living in the middle of the Pacific Ocean is in danger of dying through lack of water. It is true! A fish's blood has a lower salinity than the surrounding sea water. Water always moves from low to high salinity. When this process takes place through a membrane, such as a fish's gill, it is called osmosis. It causes fish living in the sea to lose water continually to their surroundings. The fish solve the problem by drinking lots of sea water. This helps them replace the water they lose but they also have to get rid of the extra salt they drink. Freshwater fish have the opposite problem. What is it? See page 151.

◀ The Dead Sea is really a saltwater lake. It lies 1,286 feet below sea level. It is fed by the River Jordan but it has no outlet river. The River Jordan gradually brings in more and more dissolved materials and these add to the lake's salinity. Because of the hot, dry climate, much of the lake's water evaporates. This helps to increase the salinity of the water. That is why the Dead Sea is one of the world's saltiest lakes.

More about carbonic acid (p.39); salt water (p.73)

127

Oxygen

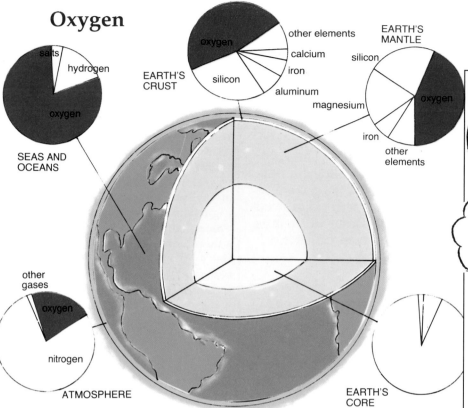

SALTS
hydrogen
oxygen

SEAS AND OCEANS

EARTH'S CRUST
oxygen
other elements
calcium
iron
aluminum
silicon

EARTH'S MANTLE
silicon
magnesium
oxygen
iron
other elements

other gases
oxygen
nitrogen
ATMOSPHERE

EARTH'S CORE

▲ Oxygen gas is part of the mixture known as air. It also combines with hydrogen gas to form water. In the Earth's crust and mantle we find it again. Here oxygen combines with other elements to form compounds known as oxides. There is no oxygen in the Earth's core.

How much oxygen?

Oxygen is the most common element on the Earth's surface. It is present in the air we breathe, in all the Earth's water and in the Earth's crust and mantle. It is present as a gas in the atmosphere but joins up, or combines, with other elements in the Earth's crust and mantle to form substances such as oxides and carbonates. For example, it forms a compound with an element called silicon which makes up more than half the Earth's crust. It also combines with hydrogen to form water.

The oxygen in the atmosphere

All living things need oxygen to carry out their daily life processes. Without it they soon die. But plants are also producers of oxygen. They give off oxygen during the day as part of the process of making food, which we call photosynthesis. This is how the Earth's atmospheric oxygen has built up over millions of years. It has been gradually "pushed" into the atmosphere by plants.

Oxygen in water

Two thirds of the Earth's surface is covered by water.

And water is made up of hydrogen and oxygen.

Every molecule of water contains two atoms of hydrogen and one atom of oxygen. You can imagine how much oxygen there is in the Earth's lakes, rivers and oceans. But most of it is combined with hydrogen. Oxygen also dissolves in water. Every 100 cubic inches of water contains 4 cubic inches of oxygen. Oxygen dissolves more easily in cold water than warm water. This is why the world's colder seas and oceans contain larger numbers of animals, including fish.

Oxygen high up

Most of the oxygen in the atmosphere is found quite close to the Earth's surface. The farther up a mountain you climb, the less oxygen you find. This is why mountain climbers on very high mountains have to take their own oxygen supplies with them. At very high altitudes, there is not enough oxygen to keep them alive.

Oxygen and burning

When things burn, the process is called combustion. A coal fire is an example of combustion. The process of burning needs oxygen and it cannot take place without it. If you cut off the oxygen supply to a fire, it soon goes out. If you give a fire more oxygen, it burns brighter and more fiercely. Burning releases energy and this can happen only when there is plenty of oxygen. This is why living things need oxygen. It is used to help them release energy from their food. Even this is a kind of "burning" process.

Oxide combinations

Oxygen combines with many other elements to form substances called oxides. Metals are found combined with oxygen to form oxides in the Earth's crust. The most common of these is aluminum oxide. When another element combines with oxygen, scientists call the process oxidation. Oxidation means joining with, or taking on, oxygen. The element is said to be oxidized.

What do you get when carbon is oxidized?	What do you get when hydrogen is oxidized?

Answers on page 151.

Oxygen can also be taken away from such an oxide. This process is called reduction. Metals can be separated from their oxides. Iron, tin, nickel and zinc are all produced by removing oxygen from their oxides.

Peat

Sometimes there is not very much oxygen around. In clay, the soil particles are packed so tightly together that there is not much room for air to circulate between them. This is especially true when the soil becomes waterlogged. Mud often does not have much oxygen. Deep-sea sediments are the same. Peat forms in poor oxygen conditions. It is produced from decaying plant material when there is not enough oxygen in the soil for the decay bacteria to survive. Peat is still used as fuel in some parts of the world.

Ozone

Sometimes oxygen atoms join up in groups of three rather than two. When this happens, a new substance called ozone is produced. Ozone is found in the stratosphere layer of the atmosphere. It provides a protective shield against too much ultraviolet radiation from the Sun. Without ozone, life could not exist on the Earth's surface.

More about ozone (pp.78, 79); the Earth's atmosphere (pp.78, 79)

Metals around the world

Mostly metal

The Earth contains about a hundred different elements or substances, and from these, all chemical compounds are made. About seventy of these elements are metals, while the rest are nonmetals or, in a few cases, halfway between metals and nonmetals.

▲ This is a piece of metal ore called pyrites. Can you guess why it is sometimes called "fool's gold?"

Comparing densities

Metals have different densities. Scientists compare the densities of different metals. The standard they use is the density of water. This kind of comparison is called relative density. Water has a density of 1. The lightest metal is called lithium. Its relative density is 0.5. This means it is less dense than water. In fact it is only half as dense as water. Gold is one of the densest metals. It is more than 19 times heavier than water.

Because metals have different densities, they are used for different jobs.

Metallurgist's Notebook

A scientist who studies metals is called a metallurgist.

1 Metals are solid at normal temperatures.
2 They can be bent easily.
3 They are usually grayish in color.
4 The surface of a freshly cut metal is shiny.
5 Metals are good conductors of heat and electricity.

Metal ores

Most metals are found in rocks combined with other elements such as oxygen, carbon and sulfur. They form carbonates when they are joined with carbon and oxygen, sulfides when they are joined with sulfur. These substances are called metal ores.

Metal partnerships

Metals can be divided into two groups. These are pure metals and alloys. Metals such as gold, copper and tin are pure metals. Alloys are mixtures of metals made by mixing two molten metals together. Brass is an alloy of copper and zinc. Bronze is an alloy of copper and tin.

Getting hold of metals

Many metals are found combined with oxygen to form ores called metallic oxides. In order to obtain a pure metal, it has to be separated, or removed, from its ore. This process is called extraction. There are two main ways of separating a metal from its ore. One is by a process called smelting. In this case, a metal ore is heated in a furnace with plenty of carbon. The oxygen in the metal oxide separates from the metal and joins on to the carbon to form carbon dioxide. This leaves the metal free. Sometimes metals are extracted by a process called electrolysis. In this method, an electric current is passed either through a solution of the ore in acid or a molten mixture of ores, and the metal is separated off.

▲ This is a bauxite mine. Bauxite is used in the manufacture of aluminum.

Looking for metals

Many of the world's metal deposits were discovered by luck. Prospectors stumbled on them by chance. Now geologists and metallurgists find metal deposits by more scientific methods. They use air and satellite photographs to analyze rocks for their metal content. They also use seismographs to gather more information about underground rocks. Geologists drill down to great depths in rocks below the Earth's surface to find out what metals they contain.

Digging for metals

Metals are obtained by mining the Earth's crust. Once geologists have found metal deposits in rocks, they have to decide the best way to get the metals out. Sometimes the mining is carried out on the surface. This is called open-cast mining. Other mines are dug deep into the Earth's crust. The metal ores are then brought to the surface so that the metals can be extracted.

Did you know?

If you heat a metal to a high enough temperature, it will boil and turn into a gas.

If all the gold that has ever been mined was gathered together, it would fit into an average-sized four-bedroom house.

Scientists sometimes analyze plants because traces of metals in their cells may provide clues to important metal deposits in the ground where they are growing.

More about relative densities (p.119); oxides (p.129)

The world of carbon

Carbon in the air

The Earth's atmosphere is made up of a number of gases, including carbon dioxide. Only 0.03 percent of the air we breathe is carbon dioxide. Even so, it is a very important gas, and the carbon it contains is a very important element.

Carbon does the rounds

Carbon forms part of the body structure of all living things. The carbon story starts with plants. They use the carbon in the carbon dioxide in the atmosphere to make their own food. We call this process photosynthesis. The amount of carbon dioxide in the atmosphere hardly ever changes. This means it must also be returned to the atmosphere. The carbon cycle does this.

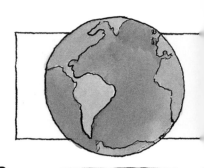

The carbon cycle makes sure the Earth's carbon is shared around easily.

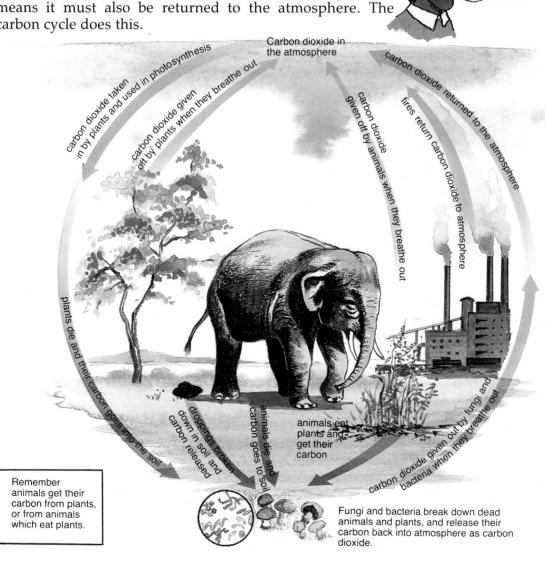

Carbon dioxide in the atmosphere

carbon dioxide taken in by plants and used in photosynthesis

carbon dioxide given off by plants when they breathe out

carbon dioxide given off by animals when they breathe out

carbon dioxide returned to the atmosphere

fires return carbon dioxide to atmosphere

plants die and their carbon goes into the soil

droppings broken down in soil and carbon released

animals die and carbon goes to soil

animals eat plants and get their carbon

carbon dioxide given out by fungi and bacteria when they breathe out

Remember animals get their carbon from plants, or from animals which eat plants.

Fungi and bacteria break down dead animals and plants, and release their carbon back into atmosphere as carbon dioxide.

132

Borrowing carbon

Animals and plants only "borrow" carbon. Some is returned to the atmosphere quite quickly when living things breathe out. Sometimes the return takes longer, and the carbon is returned only after the animal or plant dies. Sometimes the carbon is locked away from the atmosphere for millions of years before it is put back. Think about coal and oil. Peat formation puts carbon "out of action" for a long time as well.

▲ Fossil fuels like coal and oil contain carbon which has been stored for millions of years. When will it return to the atmosphere?

▲ Diamonds and coal may not look very similar. Imagine wearing a coal necklace! In fact, coal and diamonds are both types of carbon.

There are two types of carbon in the air. One type is radioactive; the other is not. A radioactive substance gives out tiny particles which we can measure. Geologists think that the amount of radioactive carbon compared to ordinary carbon has always been the same. When an animal or plant dies, its body contains a certain amount of radioactive carbon-14. Radioactive materials slowly decay or break down. This means that fossils have a "time clock" built into them. We can measure the amount of carbon-14 left in them, and work out how old they are.

Carbon forms all kinds of compounds

Carbon can form many different kinds of compounds (substances made up of more than one element) by joining with other elements. Because of the structure of the carbon atom, it can join easily with other carbon atoms. When this happens, long chains of molecules are formed, rather like joining paper clips end to end. Petroleum, kerosene and other oils are formed like this. These compounds also contain lots of hydrogen atoms. This is why they are called hydrocarbons. Carbon also joins up with metals and oxygen to form compounds called carbonates. Limestone is a compound of calcium, carbon and oxygen. Limestone rocks are found in many parts of the world.

—Did you know?—

Some of the carbon in the carbon dioxide you breathed in today may once have been part of a dinosaur 100 million years ago!

More about radioactivity (pp.33, 117); carbon dioxide (p.78)

The Earth in its place

Not the center of the universe

Until a few centuries ago, people thought the Earth was the center of the universe. Astronomers drew charts showing the Earth in the center, and the Sun, Moon and planets revolving around it. But when telescopes were invented and astronomers could make accurate measurements of the stars, they realized their mistake. In 1543, the Polish astronomer Copernicus was the first to suggest that it was the Earth and the planets that revolve around the Sun.

Worlds within worlds

The Earth is just one of nine planets which circle the Sun. The Sun, the planets and some other bodies, such as comets and asteroids, make up the solar system. The stars that we see in the night sky are also suns. Our own Sun is simply a star. Stars are extremely hot, and produce their own light and heat. Although our Sun is 864,000 miles in diameter, it is not a particularly large sun.

Quasars

Quasars are strange structures. They appear as starlike points of light, but they give off enormous amounts of energy. Some quasars produce light; others produce energy in the form of radio waves or X rays. Astronomers do not yet understand exactly what they are. Quasars are less than one billionth of the size of a normal galaxy, yet they produce as much energy as a thousand galaxies.

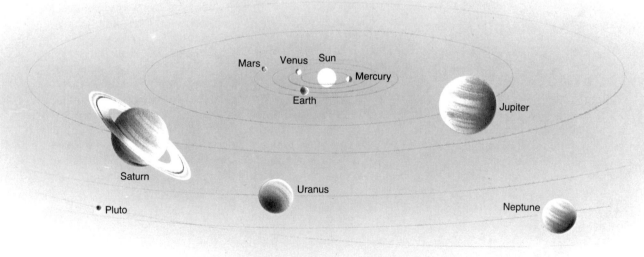

If you look up into the sky on a very dark night, you will see a misty band stretching right across it. This is the Milky Way. If you look at the Milky Way with binoculars or a telescope, you will find that it is made up of stars. The Milky Way is a huge revolving mass of about 200 billion stars, or suns, called a galaxy. It is part of a cluster of 20 to 30 galaxies. Beyond this cluster, there are many more. Astronomers think the universe contains more galaxies than there are stars in the Milky Way.

▲ The Earth is one of nine planets circling the Sun. Most of these planets move in orbits (paths) which all lie in the same plane. Only Mercury and Pluto have tilted orbits.

The Milky Way

Our galaxy is like a flattened disk with spiraling arms of stars, gas and dust, slowly circling through space. From the Earth, we are looking at this disk sideways, so it looks like a narrow band of stars. Together with our Sun, we slowly circle the center of the disc, moving round it once every 220 billion years.

▲ Our galaxy seen from the side. The center of the disk is fatter than the sides, so from this angle it looks rather like two fried eggs put back to back. Our Sun is marked X.

▲ Most galaxies are like whirlpools and are called spiral galaxies. Our own galaxy is a spiral galaxy. This is a picture of the M81 spiral galaxy.

Light-years away

The distances in the universe are so enormous that it is difficult to imagine them. If we were to measure them in miles, we would be dealing in very long numbers. Instead, we measure distance in light-years. A light-year is the distance a ray of light would travel in a year — 5.9 trillion miles.

Light travels very fast indeed. It travels 186,000 miles in a second. It can travel around the Earth in 0.125 second, from the Earth to the Moon in 1.25 seconds, and from the Earth to the Sun in just over 8 minutes. Light takes only 11.5 hours to cross the whole solar system. Our galaxy, the Milky Way, is almost 100,000 light-years from one end to the other.

Did you know?

If you were to travel at 60 mph, it would take you 177 years to reach the Sun.

Some of the stars we see in the night sky are so far away that the light we see coming from them has taken billions of years to arrive. We are looking at them as they were billions of years ago.

More about light-years (p.89); radio and X rays (p.97)

The Earth's neighbors

The solar merry-go-round

The center of the solar system is the Sun. It supplies light and heat and other forms of energy to the rest of the system. The nine planets travel around the Sun, each following its own special circular path, called an orbit. Some of the planets have even smaller spheres orbiting around them. These are the satellites, or moons. Between the orbits of the planets Mars and Jupiter, there is a belt of orbiting rocks called asteroids. Asteroids are lumps of rock of various shapes and sizes, each of which follows its own orbit around the Sun.

Almost all the orbits of the planets and asteroids lie in the same plane. Only those of Mercury and Pluto are different. So the solar system is shaped like a flat disk.

The spinning spheres

The planets are large, almost spherical bodies of rock and gas. Each planet is constantly spinning around an imaginary line drawn through its center, called the axis. The Earth spins around a line drawn through the North and South Poles. Some of the larger moons and asteroids are also spherical, but the smaller ones are all sorts of shapes. Most planets and asteroids spin round their axes in the same direction, counterclockwise when viewed from the Earth's North Pole.

A very special planet

If you could stand on another planet and look at the Earth, you would see a green and blue planet, with white poles, half hidden in swirling clouds. The Earth is the only planet in the solar system where living things are found. Although scientists believe there must be other solar systems in the universe, they have not yet been able to detect them.

The Earth is just far enough away from the Sun for water to exist as a liquid, rather than as a gas or as ice. The clouds protect the Earth from getting too hot or too cold. All living things need water and warmth. They are all killed by too much heat.

Pluto   Neptune   Uranus   Saturn   Jupiter   Mars Earth Venus Mercury

Sun

▲ This picture shows the comparative sizes of the nine planets and the Sun.

Earth's cousins

The four planets nearest the Sun — Mercury, Venus, Earth and Mars — have many features in common. They are made up mostly of rock and metal, and are quite small.

▲ Martian landscape

Mercury, the smallest planet

Mercury, the planet nearest to the Sun, is only 3,031 miles in diameter, not even half as big as Earth. Mercury is too small to have enough gravity to hold on to an atmosphere, which would protect it from extremes of heat and cold. When the Sun is overhead, it is extremely hot, about 698°F. At night, the temperature falls to −290°F. Its surface is covered in meteorite craters.

Venus, the cloudy planet

Venus is the brilliant white star seen early in the evening and around dawn. It is surrounded by clouds of sulfuric acid vapor, carbon dioxide and nitrogen gases. This prevents heat escaping into space, so the surface of Venus is very hot, around 878°F, too hot for water to remain liquid. Beneath the clouds are rolling hills up to half a mile high, many craters, and at least one giant volcano 6 miles high.

Mars, the red planet

Mars is more like the Earth than any other planet. It is smaller than the Earth, and has lost most of its atmosphere. What is left is mainly carbon dioxide gas. Mars has almost no water. With little atmosphere to retain the warmth, it gets very cold at night, as low as −202°F. In the past it probably had rivers, but today the surface is a red dust desert with craters and extinct volcanoes. Like the Earth, Mars has ice caps at each pole. In winter another kind of ice forms: carbon dioxide gas freezes to form even larger "ice" caps. Mars has two small satellites, or moons, called Deimos and Phobos.

—Did you know?—

Every spring, a dust storm starts on Mars. It spreads over almost the whole planet, and lasts for several months.

Each day on Venus lasts 243 Earth days, while a Jupiter day lasts less than 10 hours.

Unlike the stars, the planets do not produce any light of their own. They simply reflect the light of the Sun.

The minor planets

Between Mars and Jupiter lies a wide belt containing thousands of minor planets or asteroids. These are pieces of rock ranging from under a half mile to 600 miles in diameter. The larger ones are more or less spherical, but the rest have very odd shapes. Their surfaces are covered in scars and craters where meteorites have crashed into them. The rocks they are made of are similar to those found in the planets. Astronomers think they were left over from the formation of the planets.

More about the Sun (pp.142, 143); meteorites (pp.139, 144)

The birth and death of a star

Matter — attraction unlimited

Matter (the material of which the universe is made) is made up of many tiny particles. These attract each other. The bigger the particle, the more strongly it attracts other particles. This attraction is called gravity.

A star is born

No one knows for sure how the Sun and the planets were formed. Scientists believe a star begins life as a huge cloud of gas and dust called a nebula. This cloud is made mostly of hydrogen, a very light gas.

▲ A nebula — the birthplace of stars. The Orion nebula.

A nebula starts to collapse as the gas and dust particles move closer and closer to each other under the influence of gravity. Gradually the nebula shrinks to form a protostar (the beginning of a star). The pressure of the concentrating gases heats up the center of the protostar until the gases there reach about 1,800,000°F. Stars the size of our Sun take around 50 million years to get to this stage. Smaller stars take longer.

Middle age

Once the gas cloud reaches 1,800,000°F, the hydrogen atoms join together to form helium, a heavier gas. The nuclear fusion reactions produce a lot of energy in the form of light rays, radio waves, X rays, and other types of radiation. The star becomes even hotter, and the heat energy helps the hot gases to overcome the pull of the core's gravity and expand. The nuclear fusion reactions spread outward from the core, and the star becomes brighter and bigger, although its core is shrinking as the hydrogen is used up. A star the size of our Sun has enough hydrogen "fuel" to keep it going for about 10 billion years.

Giants and dwarfs

When a star reaches a temperature of about 212 million degrees F, a new kind of reaction begins. The helium atoms fuse together to form carbon. The star starts to glow bright red. It is now called a red giant. Once all the hydrogen "fuel" is used up, gravity takes over again, and the star collapses to form a white dwarf. White dwarfs are very small, extremely dense stars. The matter they contain is packed so tightly that a matchbox full would weigh several tons. The white dwarf slowly cools and fades to become a black dwarf. Finally it becomes cold and dies.

Black holes

Black holes are places in the universe where the pull of gravity is so strong that it sucks in everything around it. As gases fall into a black hole, they give off energy, often in the form of X rays. This is how astronomers detect black holes. Astronomers think a black hole is formed when an extremely large star collapses. Its center becomes so dense that not even light can escape from the pull of its gravity. No one knows what happens to materials that disappear into a black hole.

Supernovae

In some very large stars, the nuclear fusion reactions get out of hand. The star explodes, shooting matter out into space to form a cloud of dust and gas called a supernova.

Ancient craters

▲ The surface of Mercury.

The surfaces of Mercury, Venus, the Moon and the asteroids (small, rocky planets) are covered in craters where meteorites have crashed into them. Meteorites are large pieces of rock which scientists think were formed at the same time as the planets. A large proportion of these craters are about 4 billion years old. This means there were far more meteorites around then. We believe that the Sun and planets were formed at about this time.

Where did the planets come from?

Astronomers think the Sun and the planets were formed from the same swirling nebula about 5 billion years ago. Some believe the nebula broke up into several areas of gas, which eventually collapsed to form the planets.

Others think the planets were formed by separate particles colliding with each other and joining together to make bigger and bigger particles. As the particles grew in size, their increasing gravity attracted still more particles, until they became planets. The same process formed the smaller members of the solar system, the asteroids and satellites, or moons.

More about X rays (pp.96, 97); matter (p.118)

Moons, rings and gas giants

Gas giants

The outermost planets of the solar system — Jupiter, Saturn, Uranus and Neptune — are quite different from those which are closest to the Earth. Instead of being made up chiefly of rock, they are vast clouds of gases surrounding a core made mostly of liquid hydrogen and helium. These planets are enormous. The largest, Jupiter, is more than ten times the size of the Earth.

Rings

Three of the four giant planets — Jupiter, Saturn and Uranus — have ring systems in orbit around their equators. The rings are made of small particles and lumps of rock. The rings were probably formed at the same time as the planets.

▲ Saturn has over 100,000 rings.

Jupiter – cold planet with a warm heart

Jupiter is by far the largest planet in the solar system. It contains two and a half times more material than all the other planets put together and has twelve moons. It is a long way from the Sun, and takes twelve years to complete one orbit.

Jupiter is extremely cold, about −162°F on its surface. It is surrounded by colorful clouds of frozen gases. Below the clouds, an atmosphere of hydrogen, methane and ammonia stretches 600 miles down to an ocean of liquid hydrogen. Deep inside the planet, the solid core reaches a temperature of 54,000°F.

▶ On the surface of Jupiter there is a large red spot, which scientists think is a giant cloud of gas called phosphine. This gas breaks down in sunlight to produce a red substance called phosphorus.

Saturn

Saturn is the second biggest planet. It is surrounded by spectacular rings made up of millions of pieces of ice-covered rock. Winds of up to 1,100 mph stir its atmosphere.

Uranus and Neptune

Both Uranus and Neptune are very cold planets with poisonous, frozen methane atmospheres. Uranus looks green when viewed through a telescope, while Neptune appears bluish.

Pluto, the outcast

Pluto is the most distant of the planets, 3.67 billion miles from the Sun. It is very much smaller than its gaseous neighbors. In fact, Pluto is smaller than the Moon. Even so, it has its own moon, Charon. Pluto is probably made up of frozen water, ammonia and methane.

Moons and satellites

All the planets except, Mercury and Venus, have natural satellites, or moons, revolving around them. Some of these moons, like our own, are the size of planets. They, too, are more or less spherical, and spin on their axes. Other moons have strange shapes. Some are only about a mile across.

Many of these moons are rocky. Their surfaces are covered in meteorite craters. Others are glassy smooth. Some are made of rock, others of ice and frozen gases. Many moons are cold and lifeless, but some are alive with erupting volcanoes. Moons which are quite large in relation to their parent planets can have a powerful effect. Our Moon's gravity pulls the water in the Earth's oceans into tides twice a day. Astronomers think most of these moons were formed at the same time as their parent planets. A few may be asteroids that were "captured" by the planet's gravity.

Lunar landscape

The surface of our Moon is covered in meteorite craters. Some are surrounded by steep walls rising 20,000 feet above the crater floor. There are large mountain ranges, with jagged peaks over 33,000 feet high. The dark patches you see from Earth are the "seas" — dry plains of lava lying in shallow basins.

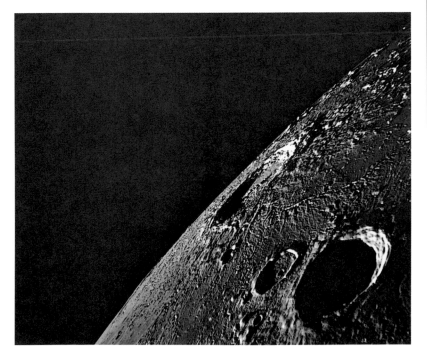

The Man in the Moon

The Moon takes 27.3 days to circle around the Earth. It takes exactly the same time to spin on its axis, so it always has the same side facing the Earth. Some people think this side looks like a man's face.

You can see some of the detail of the Moon's surface with the naked eye, but with binoculars or a telescope you get a very good view. It is fun to get a map of the Moon and try to identify the different craters and "seas."

—Did you know?—

Saturn has more than twenty moons, or satellites.

The pull of the Moon's gravity slows the Earth's rotation by 0.02 of a second every century. This means that our days are gradually getting longer.

More about tides (p.74); solar system (pp.134, 135)

141

The Sun

The center of the solar system

Our Sun is a huge globe of gas, 864,000 miles in doameter, 109 times the size of the Earth. It contains 330,000 times more material than the Earth. This gives it a powerful gravity, strong enough to hold all the planets in their orbits, even Pluto, almost 3.67 billion miles away.

Light, heat and other kinds of radiation from the Sun reach all the planets. Each planet travels in an oval path (orbit) around the Sun once a "year." The Earth's year lasts 365 days. Distant planets with very long orbits have very long years. Pluto's year lasts for 248 Earth years.

As a planet spins on its axis, a particular point on its surface spends only part of its time facing the Sun. This causes the different light and temperatures of day and night.

▲ When the Moon passes between the Sun and the Earth, it causes an eclipse. During a total eclipse. Then the Sun's corona is clearly visible.

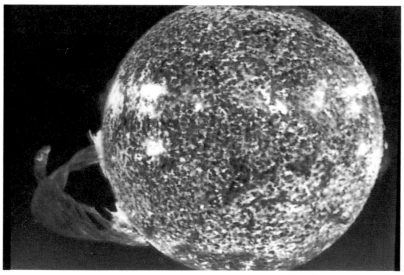

▲ The Sun, showing sunspots and solar prominences.

Inside the Sun

The Sun is made up of gases, mostly hydrogen and helium, the two lightest substances known. The center of the Sun, called the core, is its "nuclear reactor" which produces energy by converting hydrogen into helium. This energy is mainly in the form of gamma rays and X rays. It flows out from the core, and eventually reaches the outer layers of the Sun, where some of it changes into light energy. All this energy heats up the Sun's gases, and they stream toward the surface. The surface you see is one of glowing gases, with a temperature of about 10,500°F.

Sunspots

Sunspots, or solar storms, are dark spots on the Sun's surface. They can be several times larger than the Earth. Most sunspots last for about two weeks before disappearing.

Sunspots appear dark because they are almost 3,600 degrees colder than the rest of the Sun's surface. Scientists think they are caused by magnetic disturbances, which prevent hot gases rising to the surface. When sunspots are very active, the solar wind is stronger than usual and there are more solar flares.

The number of sunspots varies from year to year. They appear to have an 11-year cycle, with the total number of spots increasing to a peak, then declining again.

The solar wind

The outermost part of the Sun is the corona, a thin layer of superheated gases. Electrically charged gas particles stream out from the corona into space at speeds of around 300 miles a second. They form the solar wind.

The solar wind takes about four days to reach the Earth. From time to time, particularly when sunspots are at their peak, the Sun's gases explode with tremendous force, causing extra strong gusts of the solar wind. This interferes with radio communications on Earth, causes power cuts, and upsets compasses and computers. The solar wind affects electrically charged particles in the Earth's upper atmosphere, producing brilliant displays of colored lights in the polar skies, called the aurora.

▲ The aurora borealis, or northern lights.

Flares and flames

From time to time, violent explosions send shock waves surging across the Sun. Glowing solar flares of gas shoot out far into space. Within a few hours, all is calm again.

Other flamelike clouds of luminous gases are the "prominences." They are not flames, but are made of glowing hydrogen gas. Some of them tower hundreds of thousands of miles above the surface of the Sun. Prominences may last only a few minutes, or they may last for months.

DANGER!

Never, never try to look directly at the Sun. Its light will blind you. Dark glasses do not cut out enough of the Sun's harmful rays. Dark filters over telescopes can crack without warning as the Sun's heat is focused on them.

A billion billion suns

The stars that shine in the sky at night are all suns, more or less like our own Sun. They produce vast amounts of light, heat and other forms of energy from chemical reactions in their centers. These reactions are like those that take place in nuclear power stations. The reactions in our Sun raise its temperature at the core to about 60 million degrees F.

Did you know?

Energy produced in the center of the Sun can take a million years to reach the surface.

Every second, the Sun sheds more than a million tons of matter into the solar wind.

More about aurora (p.79); nuclear energy (p.115)

143

The night sky

The revolving sky

If you watch the sky throughout the night, you will find that the stars appear to move around the sky. They still stay in the same positions in relation to each other, but it is as if they are on a large revolving dome. It is really the Earth, not the sky, which is moving as it spins on its axis.

You can trace the path of the stars by making a photograph. If you point your camera lens at the sky directly above you and leave the shutter open for a few hours, the stars will appear on the film as curved streaks.

Shooting stars

On most nights you have a good chance of seeing shooting stars — stars which shoot rapidly down through the sky toward the horizon. They are not stars at all, but meteors. Meteors are particles of rock from outer space (extra-terrestrial rocks) which glow as they burn up in the Earth's atmosphere. Meteors probably separate from asteroids and comets which are breaking up, then come under the influence of the Earth's gravity. Most of them are very small. A speck of rock only .04 inch in diameter moving at 45 mph can glow brightly enough to form a shooting star.

Occasionally larger extra-terrestrial rocks, called meteorites, fall to the ground, making huge craters. Because of their size, meteorites do not completely burn up in the Earth's atmosphere. Many of the planets and their moons are covered in meteorite craters. The Earth does not have so many, because it is protected by its atmosphere.

Patterns in the sky

On clear nights the sky appears to be full of stars. Each star is really a sun rather like our own. For thousands of years, astronomers have tried to find patterns in the stars, to make them easier to recognize. They drew imaginary lines to join up stars. These patterns are called constellations.

Looking for planets

Although the planets shine like stars, if you look at them with binoculars, you will see that they look more like flat disks of light than twinkling dots of starlight. This is because they are much nearer than the stars. The name "planet" means "wanderer." Unlike the stars, the planets change their positions in the sky during the night, rising and setting like the Sun or Moon. They wander from constellation to constellation. Why do you think this is? Find out on page 151.

Why do stars twinkle?

Stars twinkle because their light has to pass through the Earth's atmosphere. The atmosphere is not completely steady, so the starlight gets "shaken" around.

The phases of the Moon

Full moons occur, on average, every 29.5 days. This timing is due to the combined effects of the Moon's orbit of 27.3 days, and the Earth's orbit around the Sun. The diagram below explains the phases of the Moon. How much of the Moon you see depends on the angle between the Moon and the Sun's rays. During new moons, you can see more detail of the Moon's surface, because light is reflected on to the Moon from the Earth.

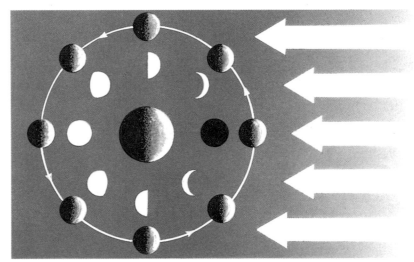

Eclipses

Eclipses of the Sun and Moon occur because light travels in straight lines. When the Earth comes between the Moon and the Sun, it casts a shadow on the Moon. In the center of the shadow, the Moon is completely blacked out. On the edges there is only a partial eclipse — the Moon looks as if someone has taken a bite out of it.

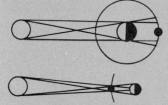

When the Moon comes between the Sun and the Earth, we get an eclipse of the Sun. Because the Sun's corona extends far into space, you can still see a ring of light during a total eclipse of the Sun.

▼ Halley's Comet photographed from Peru on April 21, 1910.

Comets

A comet is a lump of rock, ice and frozen gases that follows its own special path or orbit around the Sun. Some comets travel far beyond the farthest known planet, perhaps 10 million million miles away. They may pass the Earth only once in several million years. Encke's Comet has the shortest orbit, passing the Earth every 3.3 years.

As a comet approaches the Sun, it starts to melt, producing a glowing halo of hot gases called the coma. At this stage, it can be seen from Earth. The coma may be 80,000 miles across. The solar wind that blows out from the Sun makes many of the comet's gas particles become electrically charged, and they stream out away from the Sun in a glowing tail. A comet's tail may be up to 200 million miles long, and can stretch right across the night sky.

The particles that stream out from a comet's tail are lost forever, so a comet gradually shrinks. Eventually it breaks up altogether, forming meteor showers, and perhaps asteroids. In 1846, astronomers actually watched Biela's Comet break in two.

Worldwide quiz

What in the world are these?

Here are three different geological features. Can you name each one?

A
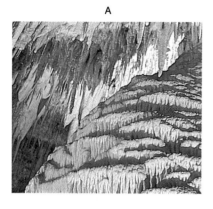

B

C

True or false?

1 Mass is the same as weight.
2 Heat is a form of energy.
3 The bending of light rays is called defraction.
4 Atmospheric pressure increases as you climb a high mountain.
5 The Sun never shines directly above the equator.
6 When you cross the International Date Line going west, you gain one day.
7 The continents were once much closer together than they are now.
8 There is more carbon dioxide in the atmosphere than there is oxygen.

Geology

1 Name the molten rock below the Earth's crust.
2 Name the pieces of rock thrown out by a volcano.
3 What is a subduction zone?
4 What kind of rock is shale?
5 What is a seismograph used for?
6 What is a caldera?
7 What is another name for gypsum?
8 What is a fault?
9 What is a cast fossil?
10 What is a batholith?
11 What kind of rock are caves mainly found in?
12 What is a hanging valley?

What's this?

Can you identify this photograph?

Cloudy. Can you name these three types of cloud?

A

B

C
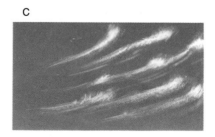

Weather forecast

Can you identify the two photographs?

A

B

Geologist's puzzle

Three geologists on a rock-collecting expedition to South America come to a branch of the Amazon River which is too wide and too deep to walk across. The river is also infested with large numbers of man-eating piranha fish. On the far bank the geologists see two young boys from the local Indian tribe which lives in the area. The boys have a small canoe with them. The canoe is big enough to carry only one geologist with his rucksack of rocks and his geological hammer, or two boys. The river is too wide to jump, and there are no tools to build a bridge. How do the three geologists cross the river safely?

Mixed bag

1 What is another name for movement energy?
2 Name the high winds which blow between the troposphere and the stratosphere.
3 Which two planets lie between the Sun and the Earth?
4 Where would you find the Sargasso Sea?
5 What name do we give to a high pressure weather system?
6 What is a spring tide?
7 Where is Old Faithful?
8 What is a tsunami?
9 How many miles is the Earth from the Sun?
10 Where would you find the Giant's Causeway?

Biggest

1 Name the world's biggest desert.
2 Name the world's largest ocean.
3 Where would you find the world's biggest bore?
4 Name the world's deepest ocean trench.
5 Name the world's highest mountain.
6 Where would you find the world's longest stalactite?
7 Name the world's largest saltwater lake.
8 What was the world's biggest bang?

Answers on page 150 – 151

147

Bookshelf

General

Planet Earth DAVID LAMBERT,
  Warwick, 1982
The Living Planet DAVID ATTENBOROUGH,
  Collins, 1984
The Hamlyn All Colour Book of the Earth KEITH LYE,
  Hamlyn, 1985
Illustrated Fact Book of Science MICHAEL DEMPSEY (Editor),
  Arco Publishing, 1983

Explainers series, Educational Development Corporation:

  Finding Out About Our Earth JANE CHISHOLM, 1982

World Geography series, Usborne:

  The Children's Book of the Earth LISA WATTS and JENNY TAYLOR, 1976
  The Children's Book of the Sea LISA WATTS and JENNY TAYLOR, 1976

Nature Library series, Time-Life Books:

  The Poles WILLY LEE and THE EDITORS OF TIME-LIFE BOOKS, 1962
  The Mountains LORUS J. MILNE, MARGERY MILNE and THE EDITORS OF
  TIME-LIFE BOOKS, 1962

Field Guides

The Golden Guide series, Western Publishing
The Peterson Field Guide series, Houghton Mifflin

The oceans

Discovering the Sea SANDRA SMITH, Stonehenge Press, 1981

Planet Earth series, Time-Life Books:

  Restless Oceans, A.B.C. WHIPPLE and THE EDITORS OF TIME-LIFE BOOKS, 1983

Planet Earth series, Bookwright Press:

  The Oceans D. LAMBERT, 1983

Geology

The Wild Edge: Life and Lore of the Great Atlantic Beaches (USA) PHILIP
  KOPPER, Penguin, 1979
The Crust of Our Earth: An Armchair Traveler's Guide to the New Geology
  RAYMOND CHET, Prentice Hall, 1983
Fossils for Amateurs RUSSELL MacFALL and JAY WOLLIN,
  Van Nostrand Reinhold, 1983
Spotter's Guide to Rocks and Minerals ALAN WOOLEY, Mayflower Books, 1979

Planet Earth series, Bookwright Press:

  *Coastlines. Volcanoes. Water on the Land. The Work of the Wind. Glaciers
  and Ice Sheets. Mountains and Earth Movements*

Easy Read series, Franklin Watts:

  Fossils NEIL CURTIS, 1984

Planet Earth series, Time-Life Books:

  *Underground Worlds. Flood. Earthquakes. Volcano. Gemstones. Continents
  in Collision. Glacier. Ice Ages. Noble Metals. Edge of the Sea*

Atmosphere and weather

The Weather Book RALPH HARDY, PETER WRIGHT, JOHN KINGTON, JOHN
  GRIBBON, Little Brown, 1982

Planet Earth series, Time-Life Books:

  Storm A.B.C. WHIPPLE and THE EDITORS OF TIME-LIFE BOOKS,
  Seventh Edition, 1982
  Atmosphere OLIVER E. ALLEN and THE EDITORS OF TIME-LIFE BOOKS, 1983

Planet Earth series, Bookwright Press:

  Weather and Climate A. and G. PURVIS, 1983

Resources

Energy Today series, Franklin Watts:

  Gas GUY ARNOLD, 1985
  Oil ALAN PIPER, 1984

Energy Today series, Franklin Watts:

  Gas GUY ARNOLD, 1985
  Oil ALAN PIPER, 1984

Young Scientist series, Silver Burdett:

  Solar Power ED CATHERALL, 1982

Science

Science Can Be Fun LOUIS BRANDES, J. Weston Watch, 1979
Crystals and Crystal Growing ALAN HOLDEN and PHYLLIS MORRISON,
  MIT Press, 1982

The Young Scientist Investigates series, TERRY JENNINGS,
  Oxford University Press, 1984

Simply Science Series, Franklin Watts:

  Radiation MARK PETIGREW, 1986
  Electricity and Magnetism KATHRYN WHYMAN, 1985

Science Club series, Lothrop, Lee and Shepherd:

  Liquid Magic PHILIP WATSON, 1983
  Light Fantastic PHILIP WATSON, 1983

Astronomy

Stargazing PATRICK MOORE, Barron Educational Series, 1985
The Universe IAIN NICOLSON and PATRICK MOORE, Macmillan, 1986
Where Will We Go When The Sun Dies? JOHN MACVEY, Stein and Day, 1983
The Lighter Side of Gravity JAYANT V. NARLIKER, Freeman, 1982
*The Children's Solar Energy Book Even Grownups Can Grownups Can
  Understand* TILLY SPETGANG and MALCOLM WELLS, Sterling Publishing,
  1982

Planet Earth series, Time-Life Books:

  The Solar System KENDRICK FRAZIER and THE EDITORS OF TIME-LIFE
  BOOKS, 1985

Planet Earth series, Bookwright Press:

  The Solar System D. LAMBERT, 1984

Answers

page 10 *Crustal plates: (i)* The volcanoes are found where different plates move together. *(ii)* You would expect to find a range of mountains where the Nazca Plate meets the South American Plate. This range of mountains is called the Andes.

Gigantic plates: You would start digging on the ocean floor.

page 12 The large land mass that you see in the photograph is the continent of Africa.

page 13 The Cetiosaurid dinosaurs probably walked to the different parts of the world where their fossils are now found. They were able to do this because the continents were joined together when these dinosaurs were alive.

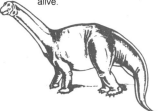

page 15 Obsidian is formed from magma that cooled so quickly that crystals did not have time to form in it.

page 21 Since the clay sediments were laid down on the sea bed, mountain-building movements have taken place in the area, which have folded the rock beds so that some of them are now vertical.

page 25 If you press down on one end, the 'rock' layers become longer and thinner, and nearby colors start to run into each other and get mixed along the borders of the layers. If you push from one side, the folds pile up and overlap each other in the direction away from your hand. The 'rocks' may even crack and split in places. If you warm the clay first, the clay folds more easily and is less likely to crack as it folds, and there is more mixing of the 'rock' layers lying next to each other.

page 31 This is a photograph of a cast fossil of a trilobite.

page 35 In order to work out the history of this rock sequence, you must start at the bottom and work your way up the right-hand side of the diagram. This is the side where you have all the layers of rock.

Starting at the bottom, there is solidified igneous rock formed from molten magma. This must have taken place after the limestone rock above was laid down, because it crosses the bedding planes of the limestone. The heat from the magma altered the surrounding rocks, changing them into metamorphic rocks.

The limestone layer is the oldest one, because it is at the bottom of the sedimentary section. This means that at the time the limestone was deposited, this area was under a shallow sea, quite near the coast. The climate must have been warm for the tiny plants and animals, whose shells form the limestone, to flourish.

Shale is formed from mud deposited in the sea. This happens a little way offshore.

Next, coal was deposited. It was formed from the undecayed remains of plants that grew in warm swamps. This suggests that the climate was still warm, but that either the land had risen or the sea level had fallen, so the area was no longer under the sea.

The evidence that sandstone was river-borne comes from the shapes of the sand grains and the pattern of the bedding. This sort of deposit is formed by a river's flood plain, as it nears the sea.

The base of the red sandstone beds cuts across rock beds of various ages. This means that it was laid down on an old erosion surface. Clearly the rocks below had been tilted since they were deposited, probably during some mountain-building period. They were then eroded, and the desert which formed the sandstone developed on the old eroded surface.

The sandstone shows cross-bedding on a large scale, which suggests that it was formed from desert sand dunes. This means a change of climate, probably to hot and dry. The area was definitely dry land at this stage.

The conglomerate that overlies the sandstone contains very smooth rounded stones, probably deposited when ice sheets covered much of the northern hemisphere over 20,000 years ago.

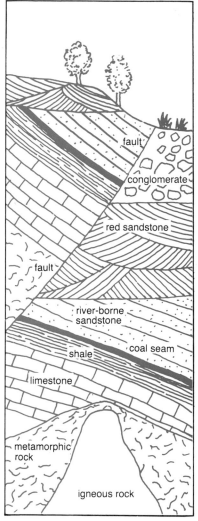

The diagonal break in the pattern of rocks is a fault. Since it cuts across rocks of all ages, it must have been formed since the youngest beds were deposited, so is due to recent Earth movements.

page 39 *Rock-splitting trees:* The roots take up water and as they grow and expand, push the rocks apart. *Did you know?* All the other rivers have gone underground, falling down widened joints in the limestone.

page 49 The thick layer of ice insulates, or protects, the ground below from the cold Antarctic air, so it is possible for water to remain above freezing point there. The water comes from deep in the rocks, moving slowly through tiny pores in the rocks.

page 78 Gravity prevents the Earth's atmosphere from floating off into space.

page 81 The airplane bumps around because it meets large numbers of water molecules and moving air currents in the cloud.

page 90 A mixture of all the different colors of the spectrum makes white light. So when you spin your top fast, the different colors appear to combine and you see white light. As your top spins more slowly and comes to rest, the different colors of the spectrum can be seen again.

page 91 A black object absorbs all the wavelengths of light from the spectrum and it reflects no light back into your eyes. Hence, it appears black. A white object absorbs no light and reflects back all the wavelengths of light from the spectrum. Hence, it appears white.

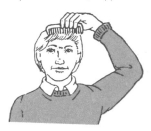

page 92 To begin with, the pieces of paper are electrically neutral. Because unlike charges attract, your strongly negatively charged comb attracts the positive charges in the pieces of paper towards it. Some of its negative charges are lost to the earth. The pieces of paper are now positively charged and 'stick' to your comb.

page 94 Mr. and Mrs. Joule discovered that the temperature of the water at the bottom of a waterfall was higher than that at the top.

page 99 10 decibels — cat purring; 30 decibels — talking quietly; 40 decibels — noise in the classroom; 60 decibels — a vacuum cleaner.

page 110 CRUNCHY POPS get their energy from the Sun. They are made from cereals which are plant seeds. The plants get their energy from the Sun when they photosynthesize. The CRUNCHY POPS seeds contain stored chemical energy.

page 111 The coal is the fossilized remains of plants which lived millions of years ago. When they were alive, these plants captured the Sun's energy. This was then stored when the plants decayed and turned into coal.

page 118 The volume of a solid cannot be changed because the atoms and molecules in a solid are packed so tightly that they cannot be packed together any more closely. Therefore, although the shape may be changed, the volume will remain the same.

page 119 An oil tanker has an overall density of less than 1. Its shape includes many compartments which contain air spaces. These reduce the ship's density to less than that of water. Hence the ship floats.

page 125 This is a picture of an Arctic iceberg. An Antarctic iceberg can be seen in the picture on page 73.

page 120 A salt crystal is cube-shaped and has six sides and twelve edges.

page 127 Freshwater fish have to take in so much water that they are in danger of bursting. They produce lots of urine to get rid of all the extra water.

page 129 You get carbon dioxide (CO_2) when carbon is oxidized. You get water (H_2O) when hydrogen is oxidized.

page 144 The planets are much nearer to the Earth than the stars that make up the constellations. It is like standing on the seashore watching the boats. A yacht that travels one mile along the coast will appear to travel much farther than a large tanker traveling one mile way out on the horizon.

WORLDWIDE QUIZ

What in the world are these: A stalactites; **B** volcano; **C** glacier.

True or false: 1 false; **2** true; **3** false; **4** false; **5** false; **6** false; **7** true; **8** false.

Geology: 1 magma; **2** tephra; **3** where an oceanic plate meets a continental plate and moves under it. It is usually a mountainous or volcanic area; **4** clay which has been subjected to pressure from overlying sediments. Under greater pressure shale turns to slate; **5** for measuring the vibrations produced by earthquakes. It is also used in oil exploration; **6** a crater where the top has been blown out of a volcanic cone by an eruption. It is also made when the rubble forming the tip of the volcanic cone collapses into the vent; **7** calcium sulfate; **8** a fracture in the Earth's crust where a mass of rock has moved up or down or sideways; **9** if a hollow left in the rocks after a dead body of an animal or plant has decayed fills up with mineral salts and turns to stone, a cast fossil is produced; **10** a magma chamber; **11** limestone; **12** a side valley left behind after a small glacier melts. It 'hangs' high above the main U-shaped valley carved by a large glacier as it slowly moves along.

What's this?: a geyser.

Cloudy: A cumulus cloud; **B** stratus cloud; **C** cirrus cloud.

Weather forecast: A a hurricane; **B** a tornado.

Geologist's puzzle: One Indian boy paddles the canoe to the three geologists on the left bank. He gets out and one geologist paddles the canoe with his rucksack of rocks and his hammer to the right bank. The geologist gets out. The second Indian boy now paddles back, collects the first boy and then returns to the right bank. This procedure is repeated until all the geologists have crossed the river.

Mixed bag: 1 kinetic energy; **2** jet streams; **3** Mercury and Venus; **4** in the mid-Atlantic Ocean; **5** an anticyclone; **6** a spring tide is when a tide is at its highest. It occurs at new moon and full moon, when both Moon and Sun are in line with the Earth; **7** Old Faithful is a geyser in the Yellowstone National Park in the United States; **8** a giant tidal wave set up by an earthquake which affects the ocean floor; **9** 93 million miles; **10** Ireland.

Biggest: 1 Sahara Desert (3.2 million square miles); **2** Pacific Ocean (64,186,300 square miles); **3** on the Ch'ient'ang'kian River in eastern China (25 feet high); **4** Mariana trench (over 36,000 feet deep); **5** Mount Everest (29,028 feet above sea level); **6** Cueva de Nerja in Spain (194 feet long); **7** Caspian Sea (141,000 square miles); **8** the volcanic eruption on Krakatoa (it was heard 3,000 miles away).

151

Glossary

absolute zero: the temperature at which all molecules stop moving. They have no heat or kinetic energy. Absolute zero is −459.67°F.

amorphous: not having any particular shape.

anticyclone: a large area of high atmospheric pressure from which all winds blow outward. It always gives settled weather over the area it covers.

asteroid: one of many small pieces of rock which move in orbits around the Sun. Asteroids are found mainly in a wide belt between Mars and Jupiter.

atom: the smallest part of any chemical element that can exist and that has all the properties of that element. All matter is made up of different atoms.

axis: an imaginary straight line around which an object spins or seems to spin. The Earth's axis passes through both the North and South Poles.

bedding plane: this is found where a layer of sedimentary rock has formed on top of another. It is the join between the two layers. Rocks are more easily split along their bedding planes.

caldera: a crater formed in a volcano after the volcanic cone has been blown away by an eruption. Sometimes the tip of the volcanic cone collapses into the vent. This also forms a caldera.

carbon dioxide: one of the gases in air. It is made up of carbon and oxygen. It is given out by animals and plants. When any carbon-bearing substance burns, it also gives out carbon dioxide. Plants use carbon dioxide to help make their food materials.

center of gravity: the point of a body around which its weight is evenly balanced or distributed.

centripetal force: the inward force that keeps a body, such as a satellite, moving in a curved path around a center. It depends on the mass of the body, its distance from the center and the speed of the movement.

chemical energy: the form of energy that is stored in a substance. It can be changed into another form of energy by a chemical reaction.

compound: a substance which contains two or more different chemical elements. The elements are held together by chemical bonds.

condensation: the process of changing a gas into a liquid by cooling it. Water vapor in the atmosphere condenses to form clouds.

conductor: a material or substance which carries or transmits energy. A copper wire conducts electrical energy. Metals conduct heat energy.

constellation: a group of stars which form a pattern or shape in the sky which we can recognize.

continental drift: the slow movement away from each other of the large continental land masses.

continental shelf: a shelf of land beneath the ocean. The shelf slopes gently away from the coast until it meets the steep continental slope.

convection: the movement of heat in a liquid or gas. The hot liquid or gas rises to the top and the cold sinks to the bottom.

crevasse: a deep crack in thick ice or in a glacier.

crustal plate: part of the Earth's crust. The crust is divided into several huge crustal plates which float and move on top of the hot liquid rock (the mantle).

current: the flow of electricity along a wire. The movement of a liquid or gas in a particular direction.

decibel (dB): a measure for comparing the loudness of sounds. Sounds louder than 140 dB can cause pain and may damage hearing.

deep-sea trench: one of the deepest parts of the oceans. Deep-sea trenches occur near the margins of continents. They mark the points where the ocean floor is being forced under the continents.

delta: a triangle-shaped area of sediment deposited at the mouth of a river where it enters a lake or the sea.

density: the mass of a substance compared with its volume. The density of water is 1 gram per cubic centimeter.

depression: an area of low atmospheric pressure.

dew: small drops of water that are formed on surfaces when warm air cools.

dew point: the temperature at which dew forms when the atmosphere is saturated with (full of) water vapor.

displacement: the weight or volume of a liquid that is pushed aside or displaced by a solid object when the object is placed or submerged in the liquid.

dissolve: to make a solid substance or a gas break up and disappear into a liquid, forming a solution.

electric charge: the amount of electricity held within something.

electrical energy: a form of energy. Electrical energy is stored as an electrical charge. This can be made to flow as an electric current. Electrical energy can be produced from other forms of energy.

electromagnetic spectrum: the range of waves which combines electric and magnetic forces that are radiated through space. Light waves are the part of the electromagnetic spectrum which we can see. Radio waves, ultraviolet rays, infra red rays, X rays, microwaves and gamma rays are all part of the electromagnetic spectrum, but all these are invisible.

electron: a tiny particle of matter which travels in orbit round the nucleus of an atom. It has a negative electric charge.

electrolysis: the breaking down of a substance in a solution by passing an electric current through the solution. In industry, metals are sometimes separated from their ores by electrolysis.

element: a simple substance made up of only one kind of atom. An element cannot be broken down further by a chemical change.

erosion: the gradual wearing away of rocks by the action of wind, rain, rivers, ice and the sea.

extinct: no longer alive or existing. Dinosaurs are extinct animals. Also, no longer active. A volcano which has not erupted for many years is said to be extinct.

fault: a fault occurs in the Earth's crust where a mass of rock has broken and moved up or down or sideways.

field of gravity: a region where gravity forces are active.

flood plain: the wide, flat area of land which is flooded from time to time by a river as it nears the sea.

fossil: the hardened remains of a dead animal or plant found in rock.

fossil fuel: fuels such as coal, oil or natural gas formed from the remains of living organisms millions of years ago.

freezing point: the temperature at which a liquid changes to a solid. Different substances freeze at different temperatures.

frequency: the number of vibrations per second in a wave pattern. The greater the frequency of sound waves, the higher the sound pitch. Also, the number of times something happens within a given time.

friction: the force that slows down movement and produces heat when two surfaces move over each other. Rough surfaces produce more friction when rubbed together than smooth surfaces.

galaxy: a huge system of stars, planets, dust and gases in outer space.

gamma rays: part of the electro-magnetic spectrum. A harmful radiation of very short wavelength. Gamma rays come from outer space and from radioactive materials.

geothermal energy: energy which comes from heat deep inside the Earth. Hot-water springs and geysers are examples of geothermal energy.

geyser: a natural hot spring that shoots hot water and steam up into the air at intervals.

glacier: a slow-moving river of ice.

granite: a type of igneous rock with large crystals, formed from hot, liquid rock.

gravity: the invisible force by which a large body attracts a smaller one. The Earth, Moon and other bodies in space exert a force of gravity. A stone thrown up in the air is pulled back to Earth by the force of gravity. Gravity gives objects weight.

Greenwich Mean Time (GMT): the time taken at Greenwich, London. All times in other parts of the world are compared to the time at Greenwich. They are either ahead or behind GMT. Parts of the world on the same longitude (0°) have the same time as GMT.

gyre: the ocean currents flow in certain directions. They turn to the right in the northern hemisphere, and to the left in the southern hemisphere, following great circular paths. Such a path is called a gyre.

helium: one of the rare gases in the atmosphere. It is lighter than air and is sometimes used for filling balloons and airships.

humidity: the amount of water vapor in the atmosphere.

humus: dark brown organic material in the soil produced by the decay of dead plants and animals.

hydroelectric energy: electricity produced from moving water.

hydrolysis: the breaking or splitting up of a substance by means of water.

hydrogen: the simplest chemical element. It is a gas which is lighter than air, and which burns easily. It combines with oxygen to form water.

ice ages: long, cold periods in the Earth's history when glaciers covered large parts of the Earth's surface.

igneous rock: rock formed by cooling and hardening of the hot liquid magma.

indigo: the band of very dark blue light lying between blue and violet in the visible spectrum.

infrared rays: invisible rays with a wavelength just longer than that of red light. They are part of the electromagnetic spectrum. All the Sun's heat radiation travels to the Earth through space as infrared rays.

insulator: a material or substance which stops energy escaping. The energy can be in the form of heat or electricity. Wood, plastic and rubber are good insulators.

interglacial period: a warmer period during an ice age when the ice retreats temporarily.

International Date Line: where the lines of longitude running east and west of Greenwich meet. It is longitude 180°.

isotope: an atom which is chemically the same as another atom of an element but which has a different number of neutrons in its nucleus.

kinetic energy: the energy of movement. All moving objects have kinetic energy.

latitude: a measure of how far a point is north or south of the equator. Lines of latitude are imaginary lines drawn parallel to the equator on a globe or map of the world. Latitude is measured in degrees from the equator going north and south. The equator is latitude 0°.

lava: the hot, liquid (molten) rock that gushes out of an erupting volcano or crack in the ground. It is also the name given to the hard rock formed from molten lava as it cools.

light-year: the distance traveled by a ray of light in one year. Light travels 5.9 trillion miles in one year.

limestone: a hard sedimentary rock made of calcium carbonate and some magnesium carbonate. Limestone is formed from the remains of microscopic sea animals and algae.

longitude: a measure of how far a point is east or west of an imaginary line running through Greenwich and joining the North and South Poles (longitude 0°). Lines of longitude are imaginary lines drawn on a globe or map of the world, running from north to south. They are numbered in degrees east and west of longitude 0°.

magma: the hot, liquid (molten) rock found in the Earth's mantle, just below the crust. During some volcanic eruptions, magma is forced out through the Earth's crust.

magnetic field: the region around a magnet within which its magnetic force acts. The Earth has a magnetic field surrounding it.

magnetic poles: the points north and south of the equator from which the Earth's magnetic forces arise or originate. The Earth's magnetic poles are not in the same position as the Earth's geographical poles.

mammal: a warm-blooded animal usually covered with fur or hair. The female mammal produces live young and feeds them with her own milk.

mantle: the part of the Earth between the crust and the core, that is, from about 25 miles to 1,815 miles below the surface.

mass: the amount of matter in an object.

matter: the material of which everything in the universe is made.

mechanical energy: kinetic energy and potential energy together form mechanical energy. It produces movement and does work.

metamorphic rock: rock formed when preexisting sedimentary or igneous rocks are altered by heat or pressure.

meteor: a solid body that enters the Earth's atmosphere from outer space and glows brightly as it burns up because of friction with the air, e.g. a shooting star.

meteorite: a solid body from outer space which has not been completely burned-up and which lands on the surface of the Earth or another heavenly body.

microwave: a form of electromagnetic radiation with wavelengths between those of heat waves and radio waves. Microwaves are used in radar, and also for cooking.

mid-oceanic ridge: the region on the ocean floor where two crustal plates meet.

Milky Way: the galaxy to which Earth belongs.

mineral: a natural substance in the Earth's crust which has a definite chemical composition and does not come from animals or plants.

molecule: the smallest amount of a substance that can exist by itself and still show all the properties of that substance. Molecules are made up of atoms joined together by bonds.

moon: a moon, or satellite, is a large solid body, sometimes as big as a small planet, which is in orbit around a planet.

moraine: a band of rocks transported by ice sheets or glaciers.

neap tides: the lowest tides, caused when the Sun and Moon are at right angles, so that their gravitational pulls partly cancel each other out.

neutron: a small particle with no electric charge, found in the nucleus of all atoms except hydrogen atoms.

nitrogen: a gas which makes up about 78 percent of the Earth's atmosphere. Nitrogen does not easily react with other substances. Unlike oxygen, nitrogen does not allow things to burn.

nuclear energy: the energy released during the splitting of the nuclei of atoms.

nucleus: (*pl.* nuclei) the central part of an atom, usually containing protons and neutrons.

ore: a mineral from which a metal can be extracted.

oxidation: the addition of oxygen to a substance.

oxide: a compound made up of two elements, one of them being oxygen.

oxygen: a gas which makes up nearly 21 percent of the atmosphere. The commonest element on Earth, also occurring in combination with many other elements. Water is made up of oxygen and hydrogen.

ozone: a gas occurring in the lower layers of the stratosphere. It stops most of the Sun's ultraviolet radiation reaching the Earth.

pack ice: densely packed large pieces of ice floating on the sea.

photosynthesis: the process by which plants make new living (organic) material from carbon dioxide gas and water, using the energy of sunlight.

planet: any one of the bodies in space, including the Earth, in orbit around the Sun. Also, planets in orbit around other suns.

polar reversal: when the Earth's north and south magnetic poles change places.

polarized light: light in which the light waves vibrate in only one plane.

potential energy: energy which is stored and not being used.

precipitation: the falling of water or ice in the form of rain, sleet, hail, snow, fog and mist.

prevailing wind: the wind that blows most often in a particular place and in a particular direction.

prism: a piece of glass or transparent plastic with two identical flat triangular faces separated by three flat rectangular faces. It may be used to bend rays of light and to split white light into the colors of the spectrum.

proton: an extremely small particle with a positive electric charge, found in the nucleus of all atoms.

quartz: a hard glasslike mineral, made up of silicon and oxygen.

radar: a system of navigation which uses very high frequency sound waves. The sound waves bounce off distant objects, and these reflected waves are analyzed to give information about the shape and position of the object.

radiation: the movement of energy given out in electromagnetic waves from a source, e.g. heat and light radiation from the Sun, X rays, ultraviolet radiation.

radioactivity: the giving off of harmful radiation in the form of waves and particles, such as gamma rays, when the nuclei of atoms break down.

rare gases: Gases such as helium, krypton and xenon which make up less than 1 percent of the Earth's atmosphere.

refraction: the bending of rays of light (or a wave of heat or sound) when it passes at an angle from one less dense medium to a denser medium, or vice versa.

relative density: the density of a substance compared with the density of water. The density of water is 1. More dense materials have a density greater than 1.

satellite: a body in orbit around a larger body in space. For example, the Moon is in orbit around the Earth.

sedimentary rock: rock made from material that has settled to the bottom of a river, lake, or sea, or which has been dropped by the wind.

sediment: material that has been deposited on the bed of a river, lake or sea, or on the surface of the land.

seismograph: an instrument used to study the vibrations produced by earthquakes. It is also used in oil exploration.

silicon: an element present in quartz and glass and, in combination with other elements, in rocks and soil.

silt: a sediment made up of small particles from $\frac{1}{20}$ millimeter in diameter or less.

solar: of the Sun.

solar system: a group of planets and other bodies in space revolving around a sun.

solar wind: a stream of electrically charged gas particles which blows out into space from the surface of the Sun.

spectrum: the range of different types of electromagnetic waves. The electromagnetic spectrum ranges from long wavelengths, such as radio waves, to short wavelengths, such as gamma rays. The visible spectrum is the rainbow-colored bands of light seen when white light is split up by water droplets in the atmosphere or a prism. It ranges from red to violet light.

spring tides: the highest tides, formed when the Sun and Moon line up to exert the maximum pull of gravity.

stalactite: a column of calcium carbonate hanging down from the roof of a limestone cave.

stalagmite: a pillar of calcium carbonate growing up from the floor of a limestone cave.

thermal: a column of rising air that has been heated by the hot ground below.

thermocline: in oceans and lakes, a boundary between water of fairly uniform temperature which is mixed by the wind, and cooler unmixed water below whose temperature decreases with depth.

tide: the regular rise and fall of the water in seas and oceans due to the gravitational pull of the Moon. Tides occur twice in every lunar day.

time zone: a region throughout which, by international agreement, the time is the same.

tropics: the part of the world lying between the tropic of Cancer, latitude 23° north, and the tropic of Capricorn, latitude 23° south of the equator.

ultraviolet radiation: electromagnetic rays present in sunshine, next to violet light in the spectrum. Ultraviolet rays are invisible, but act on photographic film. They cause sunburn.

uranium: a metallic element found in certain rocks. Its atoms spontaneously break down, releasing radioactivity. It is used to produce nuclear energy.

vacuum: a space that has no matter in it.

water table: the level in rocks below which the rock is saturated with (full of) water.

wave: a vibrating up and down movement of energy or particles traveling in a given direction. Light, heat and sound travel in waves. It is also the raised ridge of water along the surface of an ocean or large lake.

wavelength: the distance between the crest of one wave and the crest of the next wave.

weather front: the dividing line between the cold air of a depression (low pressure weather system) and the warm moist air of an anticyclone (high pressure weather system).

weight: the heaviness of something. The pull of gravity which attracts an object towards the Earth. The weight of an object depends upon its mass and upon its distance from the Earth's center of gravity.

X rays: electromagnetic waves with very short wavelengths. X rays can affect photographic film. In large doses they are very harmful to living organisms.

zero gravity: when an object is so far from the Earth that it is beyond the Earth's field of gravity, it is no longer affected by gravity. In such a situation objects do not fall downward — they do not fall at all.

World records

The lowest temperature ever recorded in the atmosphere is −225.4°F. It was recorded at an altitude of about 56 miles.

The greatest volcanic eruption known to have taken place was that of Tambora in Indonesia, in 1815. After the eruption, the volcano was 5,249 feet shorter.

Antarctica contains 99 percent of the world's ice.

The place with the highest average yearly rainfall is Mount Wai-'ale 'ale in Hawaii. It averages 45 inches per year.

The highest active volcano is in Argentina. It is the Volcan Antofalla which rises to a height of nearly 21,325 feet.

The world's greatest land mountain range is the Himalaya-Karakoram range. It contains 96 of the world's 109 peaks over 24,000 feet.

The world's most remote island is Bouvet Øya in the South Atlantic. It is approximately 656 miles from any other land.

The world's largest volcano crater is in central Sumatra, in Indonesia. It covers an area of 685 square miles.

The world's highest sand dunes are found in the Sahara Desert, in Algeria. They have a maximum height of 1,410 feet.

The world's biggest continent is Asia. It has an area of 17,152,878 square miles.

The longest lasting rainbow was seen in North Wales in 1979. It lasted more than 3 hours.

The world's longest estuary is the Ob' estuary in northern Russia. It is 550 miles long.

The highest sea wave ever recorded measured 112 feet high. It was recorded during a hurricane in 1933.

The biggest tsunami ever seen was estimated to be 278 feet high.

The world's largest ocean is the Pacific. It covers an area of 64,186,300 square miles, and represents nearly 46 percent of the world's oceans.